My 1

poetry today

MY FIRST . . .

Edited by
Suzy Walton

First published in Great Britain in 2001 by Poetry
Today, an imprint of
Penhaligon Page Ltd, Remus House, Coltsfoot Drive,
Peterborough. PE2 9JX

A Catalogue record for this book is available from the
British Library

ISBN 1 86226 687 5

Typesetting and layout, Penhaligon Page Ltd, England
Printed and bound by Forward Press Ltd, England

Foreword

My First is a compilation of poetry, featuring some of our finest poets. This book gives an insight into the essence of modern living and deals with the reality of life today. We think we have created an anthology with a universal appeal.

There are many technical aspects to the writing of poetry and *My First* contains free verse and examples of more structured work from a wealth of talented poets.

Poetry is a coat of many colours. Today's poets write in a limitless array of styles: traditional rhyming poetry is as alive and kicking today as modern free verse. Language ranges from easily accessible to intricate and elusive.

Poems have a lot to offer in our fast – paced 'instant' world. Reading poems gives us an opportunity to sit back and explore ourselves and the world around us.

Contents

First Kiss

Tonight,
It's all arranged,
2 American summer sweethearts
2 naïve Scottish teenage girls 'never bin kissed'
Nervous laughter,
holding hands,
dry lips breath checking
short walk back up the lane,
'*Wait!* Carole, no!'
She's chickened out,
Her date skulks off dejectedly
All alone, us two, at my door
Heart pounding, hands sweating
We stop.
'Goodnight Kate,' softly spoken
Leaning forward this is it.
Gentle, lingering, fireworks exploding in my head.
We part, he smiles, I blush
'See ya tomorrow.'
He jauntily struts down the street
I dive into the house straight onto the phone
Berating and boasting euphorically high.
So this is love.

Kate Fraser

Lip Service

I covered my first love in kisses,
On that memorable hot day in June.
My young heart was frantically racing,
I had found love so young and so soon.

At first we had eye to eye contact,
You know how your heart gladly skips.
That fantastic unrivalled sensation,
Of those tingling, eager, luscious lips.

This moment I will always remember,
Knowing what now true love this is.
That hot summer love was forever,
As my mirror was covered in kisses.

T A Napper

When I First Went To . . .

When I first went to the seaside,
I thought it was great,
I jumped right in,
Before it was too late.

When I first went to the park,
I couldn't wait,
I quickly skipped
Right through the gate.

When I first went to the fair,
There were lots of lights,
It was so cold,
I wore my woolly tights.

When I first went to the library,
It was very big,
There were so many stories,
I even saw a book called Twig.

When I first went to the shops,
It was wonderful,
I wanted a Sea Barbie,
She was so beautiful.

Eve Lester

My First Love
(Dedicated to my beautiful man, Kevin D Gregson)

We met in a pub on a Sunday night,
For both of us it was love at first sight.
We chatted a while, till I had to go home,
So I gave him my number and told him to phone.

He phoned the next day and asked for a date,
I was ready at six, he was coming at eight.
We dined in the moonlight, with the stars up above,
And I knew that I'd found my first true love.

We dated a while then we got engaged,
'It won't last!' some said, some even waged.
But we stuck it together, side by side,
And proved wrong the pessimists, and those who had lied.

We're still together now, and happily wed,
When *we* spoke our vows we *meant* what we said.
Nobody *ever* could tear us apart,
He's sill my first love who so captured my heart.

Flee

4

Undertaker's Lace

My first time was a time of woe
It happened many long years ago;
I did not know what to do
Or where to go;
I was lost but nobody knew
Left out in the cold till I turned blue;
But things got better as I grew
Although hardships I've been through;
Life has taught me from an early age
Against difficulties a battle I have to wage;
This is not always easy in my case
Because that's the way of the human race;
Others try to engineer my demise
And work towards my fall from grace;
They tell tales behind my back
But never repeat them to my face;
For people like that I care not much
They soon will be wrapped in undertaker's lace.

S Glover

The First Of My Children

The first of my children
So tiny and new,
Oh what a love I have for you.

The first time you looked
And gave me a smile,
All in my world stood still for a while.

The first steps you took,
My heart skipped a beat,
Standing alone on your own tiny feet.

Your first day at school, all on your own,
Growing so fast, the years have just flown.

The first of my children, now you have grown,
The first of your loves, you are bringing home.

Today is the day, the first day of your life,
When standing beside you, will be your wife.

So now I do pray, that you too will say,
The first of my children,
So tiny and new,
Oh what a love I have for you.

Audrey Bosworth

Untitled

The autumn turns to golden brown
As it comes, my heart does drown
Deeper, deeper as it falls
No one hears the cries, the calls
Of a dying heart that no one needs
Buried under a sea of leaves
This sea of leaves that soon will rot
And beneath, my heart, forgot
Under winter's stony ground
Still lies my heart, still unfound
But maybe years or maybe one
Someone will find, someone will come
He'll find my heart and see the pain
And try to make it beat again
He'll give it love and take it home
And make sure it is not alone
So rest weary heart, do not weep
You did not die, you're just asleep

Shelagh Persich

The Spoken Word

Why so useless with the spoken word?
That I write instead of feelings dear
I have people of whom to see
But do not see the love
Or catch a sight
Of the love, I want to see

Relax, stop questioning
I may have to let her go
My heart will break
And fail to grow
And burn in my mind's fire

I know me
Deep hidden desire
But desire is eating at my soul
And soulful, down
I will be

For better times, I hoped to see
But single not
She'll ever be.

Neil Phillips

The Words Of A New Mum!

The first time I looked at my baby,
I felt such a rush of great love.
I was certain this sweet, tiny bundle,
Was a gift sent from God up above.

No-one can imagine that moment,
When your own little miracle arrives.
The feeling is so overwhelming,
The greatest in all of our lives.

The pain of the birth was forgotten,
And I cried only tears of joy.
As he took his first breath of life,
And the midwife announced 'It's a boy!'

The first little cuddle was magic,
As I gazed down and kissed his cute nose.
I marvelled at such perfection,
As I checked all his fingers and toes.

His daddy and I were amazed at,
How close our creation had brought us.
A feeling that could only be matched by
The birth of our two lovely daughters.

Lynne Doyle

First Date

It wasn't like I thought it would be . . .
Meeting my parents; coming for tea;
Flowers and chocolates, dancing all night,
Holding my hand under the moonlight.

It wasn't like I thought it would be,
It was 'Wait for me there under that tree,
If I remember, I'll meet you at six,
Pay for yourself and we'll go to the flicks.'

It wasn't like I thought it would be,
I was cold and wondering 'Where on earth is he?'
That shouldn't happen on a first date,
Then, 'Oh, there he is and he's brought his best mate.'

Christine Karalius

Untitled

I looked at your face, and felt an overwhelming grace,
I sighed with relief for I had just received the greatest gift,
My perfect child was so beautiful,
Skin so soft and eyes so bright,
And as I heard you softly breathe,
Knew you were real and you were all mine,
For the first time in life I had succeeded,
A sudden bond - a love so strong,
Like nothing I'd ever felt before,
Like I was the magnet and you were drawing me in,
I knew from that moment,
I'd never do you wrong,
For I had found what I'd always searched for -
A love so intense, unconditional and greater than my own.

K Hall

First Affair Of My Heart

Deep within my heart I know it is wrong,
Feelings flowing that really should be gone.
Every time I see his eyes looking back at me,
I can't keep my distance I just cannot resist.
Emotions become deeper as time passes by,
Each moment we share together is more special.
Still feelings of guilt stay within my mind,
Knowing he has another eats away at me.
Words he says assure me we will be happy,
One day we will be together very soon.
Sometimes I can't help but feel doubt,
I know one chance is all I give no more.
Never in my past have I fell for a taken man,
It feels like the most impossible way to live with love.

Zoe Fitzjohn

Who Gave You That Smile?

I can recall so clearly
The very first time we met;
He thought his chat-up line was so cool.
'Say, who gave you that smile?'
I'd heard it before in some old movie
But somehow it never failed.

We married too young after a passionate romance,
Now he's no more than a stranger -
Lying in a hospital bed
Listening to that awful 'beep beep' sound.
I know that I look a mess
But if you can't see me
I know that there isn't any point,
I don't want to look pretty for anyone but you.

I didn't notice when the machine stopped
My heart was beating too loud.
I think back to all the times our friends said
That it would never last.
I guess that this has proved them right
But by God we put up a fight;
Because you gave me that smile.

Vicky Stevens

First Kiss

Walking home late from a dance
One icy November night
As if in a trance
We saw a star take flight
Across the sky
It seemed to fly
So swiftly
The moon, full and large, frosted in rime
Swung, suspended in time
My lover-to-be bent close to me
Kissing me for the first time
The air was so still and time stood still
He hugged me close to him
And in the interim
The star had fallen
I made a wish, holding my breath
And we walked on home
On the wintry, snow-covered earth

We knew it had to be
My beloved and me
A falling star and first kiss
To live on in memory.

Lilian Brereton

The First Time . . .

The pain of your fist smashing into the side of my face,
Was nearly as painful as the cold hand of fear that gripped my heart,
The first time that you hit me . . .

The pain on my father's face,
When I left home to marry you,
Was nearly as painful as when you slept with someone else,
The first time you hurt me . . .

The pain of feeling my unborn child moving in my womb,
Was nearly as painful as hearing you tell me to kill it, or you would .
. .

The pain of killing a child to save myself,
Was more pain than I could bear,
So I left you,

The first time . . .

P J Rowlands

The Ring

It's difficult choosing a ring when I don't know how much he's got
He might have very little or want to spend quite a lot
We look in the jeweller's window at all the different rings on show
If he has a price limit I wish to God he'd let me know
As we walk expectantly into the shop I feel a little scared
I have butterflies in my tummy and I feel quite unprepared
The sapphire ring with the small stones is really rather nice
But before I tell him I like it I take a glance at the price
A large diamond cluster can't help but catch my eye
But realising it's too expensive I do my best to suppress a sigh
There's a lovely diamond solitaire that's nestling in the tray
Ask the assistant if I can try it on, please if I may

As she hands the ring to me it sparkles in the light
I slip it onto my finger and am delighted it fits just right
It feels so natural wearing, it, as if it'd always been there
It's absolutely gorgeous, I can't help but sit and stare
My future husband asks me if this is the ring I like best
I nod and explain that for me it stood out from all the rest
I ask him if he thinks it's expensive and does he like it too
He says not to worry about the cost as only the best will do
And that buying a ring for your future wife
Isn't something that happens every day of your life
As he goes to the till to pay and I urge him not to linger
I can't wait to show off this ring that's weighing down my finger!

Carole Canavan

From The First

The first time that I saw you,
From that second on I knew
There were none before you
And no one would follow, too.
Each today is like tomorrow
Never knowing what's in store,
Since that first time you borrowed
My heart for evermore.
Even now, when I recall
All you said, it's like I hear
Your words; and then again I fall
In love, for you're still here.
Like the taste of deep red wine
Seeping in and keeping thoughts aglow,
I lose all sense of time:
Are we now, or long ago?
In your eyes of green, gleams
A recognition of the fact
All our schemes, hopes and dreams
Have in time been carefully packed
Away, in a way that proves
Each cliché and romantic song
Contains those plain, honest truths
We've known all along.
Though you and I have altered since,
At heart remain the same -
Pulses darting when we glimpsed
And I asked your name.
Then it was, and now it is,
From the first time till the next;
One of life's great mysteries
As simple as a page of text.

Jonathan Goodwin

My First Son

It was a special day when you were born
My darling little boy
You came into my life
And filled my heart with joy

As I gazed at you so closely
I could see you look at me
Your tiny eyes so new and bright
I feel you're part of me

Your little fingers so small
Your toes so tiny too
You're such a little treasure
I love you, yes I do

The weeks turn to months
The months to years
Our life we share together
Will be of laughter and tears

There'll be times, I know
When I'll get cross with you
When you do something naughty
As boys so often do

But when I scold you
Please remember this
I will always love you
And be ready with a kiss

If you have a problem
I'll always be there
In the years ahead
Your worries I will share

That is what a 'mum' is
To be there through thick and thin
So don't forget to open your heart
And always let me in

C A Watts

aarising

the first time i met god
i was just blood
he was the love
the first time i met god
he set the fire

the next time i met god
i was the child
his church was empty
the next time i met god
he wasn't there

the third time i met god
i lost my page
and found no caution
the third time i met god
he offered life

the last time i met god
he showed me footprints
while creating worlds
the last time i met god
he hid the dice

the next time i'll meet god
i'll be shock cold
he'll find me warm
the next time i'll meet god
we'll no longer be alone

edi little

Dancing

As we twirled and turned
The music played
Dancing
In a room full of others
I didn't notice.

The music would stop
The song was done
We sat down
And I watched him
Surreptitiously.

Friends would chat
Have a drink
And a nibble
The music would start
Again.

From across the room
I watched him
Moving
His eyes on me
Mine on him.

And I wanted to dance
With him
Forever
Those moments we shared
Everlasting.

And he took my hand
Two seven-year-olds
Dancing again
He was always to be
My first love.

With schooldays gone
All I have are
Memories
Of special times
. . . Of firsts.

Gill Webster

The Worst Hangover

The first is always the worst
You'll find that as you curse
The first is always the worst
Though the second is scarce

The first is always worst
With your head submersed
The first is always worst
With coffee as your nurse

The first is always worst
With the illusion burst
The first is always worst
The stomach has a lurch

The first is always worst
As head and ache merge
The first is always worst
A regretful mirth

The first is always worst
The room spins in the murk

You sign the oath with a pen
To never ever drink again

Andrew J Forrest

My First Bunny

My first rabbit
an incurable habit
floppy-eared
lovingly reared
cucumber-eater
nothin' sweeter
calm, timid, explorable
nature,
happiness-maker,
caring pet,
one I'll never
forget,
soft and funny,
my first bunny.

Daniel Wood (11)

The First Time I Saw Paris

The first time I saw Paris,
I was middle-aged and grey -
O would that I'd been very young,
That dull September day.

I would have wished to kiss the boys
And dally with them there;
Then gone to see the dazzling sights
Of Montmartre and Folies Bergere.

Instead I saw the Eiffel Tower;
Went sailing on the Seine;
Passed quickly through the Sacre Coeur;
Saw Champs Elysees in the rain.

The last time I saw Paris -
In far advanced old-age,
I visited Les Invalides.
Appropriately sage.

Lorna Alexander

The Music Lesson

On a waiting list I went
And when my turn had come,
You rang me up and told me
My lessons had begun.
So, a week to the day
You were true to your word,
You arrived with a smile
And from me, not a word.
The fear that gripped my body
Had taken my control,
My hands shook and trembled,
My fingers numb and cold.
Then you sat upon the stool
And started up to play,
The music taking over
I began to see the way.
I thought this is so easy
I tried to keep my cool,
And started on the lesson
Just as quickly as I could.
Although the mind is willing
The body's still in charge,
My fingers they were fumbling
My eyes were strained and large.
The half hour it was endless
The mistakes came more and more,
And instead of thinking music
I thought about the floor.
And wished that it would open
And swallow me all up,
To hide my embarrassment
At being such a flop.

Merle Jones

My Real Love

Your smile fills me with a lovely glow,
What you see in me, I'll never know.
I'm not handsome, it's plain to see,
You may find a prettier face and leave me.
But you say, you are the only one for me,
And when I look in your eyes I know it's true.
I'm so happy, I feel ten feet tall,
For we love each other, and love is all.
You are the best thing that happened to me,
The greatest love of my life.
I feel I could reach and touch the sky,
You are my love forever,
I'll love you till I die.
You have been gone a long time, but
You are always here with me,
Till we meet again some day, my love
I'll wait patiently.

G M Gill

My First Day At Work

My very first day Monday morning
I could hear the alarm screaming, calling
People dashing scattering up cold stone steps
High heels clattering leather soled reps
Workmates laughing, giggling, chattering
Typists, secretaries, cleaners bantering
Doors slamming, bosses damning
Cars screeching, elders preaching,
Seconds, minutes, then all is hush
Stood in a corridor alone, legs like mush
The silence is deadly; testing, criticising
Ice-cold stares from unknown people chastising
Standing waiting to be grilled
The air around is thin and chilled
Cannot stand the wait, heart is thumping
The whole of the nerves in my body jumping
Suddenly heavy footsteps drawing near
Echoes loudly from the rear
Turning swiftly twisting my neck
My brain now a shrinking wreck
A large broad man grabs my hand
Shakes it like a rubber band
How do you do lass my name's Jack
Let us get you girl on the right track
Giving me a smile from ear to ear
Led me through a crowd of cheers
Welcome newcomer join the clan
My first day at work as sweet as jam

Janet M Parsons

28

1952
The First Of Many

I remember vividly
The day that I left school
'Get an office job my lad,'
My father was no fool

Anyone can shovel coal
Or carry bricks and mortar
But if you get an office job
You may marry the boss's daughter

And so, on Monday morning
With waistcoat watch and fob
I found myself stood gasping
In this big office, my first job

Commissionaire, and head lad Matt
Who ran the office system
Welcomed me with open arms
The rules? I must have missed 'em?

Because of this I felt much pain
As rule on rule I broke
How was I to know the rule
That shouting was 'no joke'

The corridors vibrated
With vocal chords all strung
Stop your shouting Glinnie?
Or you will get me hung

This remark was made to me
I remember to this day
The dulcet tones of the Commissionaire
Whose name was Sammy Ray

Tommy Glynn

29

Memories - And The Cinema

My parents took me to see Snow White
And Cinderella. I sat on my mother's knee
Kissed her cheek, ate ice-cream in the messy way.
Hollywood and matchstick men.

Then Annie Get Your Gun,
I was frightened of the gun,
An awkward one I was.

But Zhivago, here at its best,
Until, I opened the pages of Pasternak,
Read Lara's Theme in poetry.

Of Puccini's Madame Butterfly,
(Dubbed by a beautiful actress),
I cried at every showing, (six times),
So beautiful, so sad.

Ballet films: The Bolshoi,
Galina Ulanova's Giselle;
Love lasting through the white mists of Hell.

And the funny ones; Carry On Doctor,
Carry On . . . all those films.
Ah, memories and films now swimming in my head.

And organ intermissions,
Rising like Poseidon in a rainbow.
And me sitting on the back row,
With that young lad, or that young lad.

Now videos: films old and new;
And you and me on the sofa sipping wine,
Arms wrapped round - a delight.

Yet, the cinema is the best place
To see a movie. Its house lights dimmed
And all the world a big wide screen.
Casablanca, Michael Collins, Romeo and Juliet.

Maureen Weldon

Big Yellow-Headed Duck And Monkeyface

Big Yellow-headed Duck
Came first
With a knowledge never known
Magic feelings
Bursting forth
From his multi-coloured down
'Feel at peace'
He said to me
The words shone from his face
'Then feel the torture
And the pain
As I join this strange rat race.'
Then Monkeyface
Came second
But first to some degree
'He may be Big Yellow-headed Duck
But I,' she said
'Am me.'

Bonnie Markham

Nan

The first time I realised you weren't coming back,
I swear, I heard, my tender heart crack.
And all because,

You were the one who made me strong,
The one who taught me right from wrong,
Always there in my hours of need,
How I loved you, how indeed.

I trusted you, you trusted me,
I miss you now, but no-one can see,
You were my strength, my whole life too,
But now you're gone, and what can I do.

But you live on in me, you're in my heart,
And nothing in this world could tear us apart,
I think about you, almost every day,
And I love you still in every way.

So although we're apart, we're together still,
And in my heart we always will,
So your memory lives on, as long as I do,
I am me, but I'm also you!

Tracy Parker

My First Bath

Bubbles in my hair,
Bubbles up my nose,
Water in my eyes,
Soap between my toes.

Bubbles on the wall,
Bubbles on the door,
Water on the towels,
Soap on the floor.

Abbie Latham (9)

Lines Written In Contemplation Of Some Portraits Of The Madonna And Child
(In the National Gallery, London)

O Thou whose star-wrought mantle clothes
   The heavens to veil their bliss,
Fair as the moon whose streaming light
   Cleaves wide the Ocean's breast,
Distilled in Thee of Spirit's breath
   Infusing earthly clay,
Brought forth by Thee, upon thy lap
   Of Time and Space I lay.

O Mother Dear, I gaze upon
   Thy love-enraptured face,
What halo of All-Holy Light!
   What glory full of grace!
Reflecting from thy Lord afar
   Beyond the pale of Night,
Whom thou canst see, Whom none can see,
   Save imaged in thy light.

I see thy surging, heaving breast
   I hear thy murmuring voice,
The zephyrs of thy lovely lips,
   My infant heart rejoice,
My head is pillowed on the hills
   Whence living fountains flow,
And fed from thy maternal depths,
   I thirst nor hunger know.

The sheen of shimmering star-dust streams
  Across thy vesture spread,
A hymeneal wisp of light, thy virgin maidenhead,
  The teeming seas in rapture poured,
All creatures came to be,
  When He who spoke rained through the veil
Betwixt Himself and thee.

William Mead

First And Best Forever

Lugano's truly lovely when all's said and done.
That's not because of scenery alone.
Simply the holiday was first not once but twice;
First after a hateful war, then first one chose, planned,
Found the price.
No more, we're going where you're told:
You'll enjoy it, put own views on hold.
But now the train runs past the first Swiss cats on parapet
          of owner's summer home with cushions set,
Then into the chestnut woods and out again
Stopping above the town with aqua lake, amethyst and
                                        emerald mountain.
Goldstone houses, shops beneath arcades held presents to take home.
One bought them, then simply went to roam.
Cathedral reached up flight of stairs;
One almost took them then in pairs.
Church with glass coffin with first bishop resting.
A close look could be a fraction testing.
Then evenings in the open Asti sipping;
New friends could send French grammar tripping.
Time to go home came all too soon,
Starting back in the sunny noon.
Travel since has been worldwide - or round.
Yet back in Lugano, first warmth can still be found.

Joanna Mackay

My Firstborn

For nine long months you grew beneath my breast,
I weaved such dreams *as only* mothers can,
For health, good fortune and the rest,
And happiness in everything you'd plan.

Joy came through travail and I cradled you
And pondered on that miracle of birth -
Your tiny form so perfect and so new
Made me the proudest human on this earth.

The transformation from the babe to man
Though gradual, seemed but only as a day,
And then, when Fate fulfilled its devious plan,
I agonised and watched you slip away.

Though passing years erode the edge of grief,
And you're at peace beneath that shady tree,
I know that, when Death turned that final leaf,
He also took away a part of me!

Joan Leahy

First Antique Impressions

Old objects precious to the eye,
Acquire beauty,
When times mellow age,
They wear,
For the charm of years,
Shall weave her story,
And entwine a history rare.
A history of Time's enchanted story,
That carries the fashion of time to shine;
Yet with every varied hue,
Holds within its grasp,
A bright reality -
Speaking of truth's finality,
Its echoes to clasp within time.

Christine Hare

My First Son
(Devoted to my son Anthony)

A precious new life had begun, when I gave birth to my very first
son,
An aura of peace shone around his head, as he lay there contentedly
on my bed,
I could not take my eyes off of him, that very first night,
Trying to take in as much as I could, of his glorious sight.

Pregnancy, labour and birth, are no amount of pain,
For the overwhelming feeling of love and happiness, that you
have to gain,
Love, care, play and attention, is all that they crave,
You teach them everything in life, like how to behave.

You watch them day by day, as they grow up,
Handing them advice, wisdom and lots of luck,
Sometimes I still stand and stare, at my beautiful son lying there,
I smile in joy at what I've done, brought into the world my
very first son.

Joanna Dicks

To My First Grandchild

My little Grandson's hand in mine,
Soft, chubby fingers intertwine,
And gently squeeze as we walk away,
'Nan, what shall we do today?'

With picture books of talking trains,
We're happy, 'though outside it rains,
We draw and colour, cut and paste,
Not a minute do we waste.

I look down on his golden head,
I see my son there instead,
The same blue eyes and happy smile,
I'm in a time-warp for a while!

He's my son's son, Adam Paul,
So many memories I recall,
Nothing more precious I command
Than the perfect trust in that little hand.

O Miller

First Love

First love must come to each young life,
Cupid's arrow, more like an assassin's knife.
Puppy love, friends say it's no big deal,
Raw feelings, naked trust, nothing's so real.

First love's like a fever, an obsession of the mind,
You can't sleep, you can't study, first love is blind.
Too young to satisfy, too innocent to know why,
Too inexperienced to understand why first love must die.

Keith Leese

The First Holiday Abroad

The black and white photograph
Taken at the station in nineteen-forty-nine.
School party to Switzerland,
Fifteen years old and leaving behind
Rationing, shortages, and bomb damage.
Surely adventure and excitement
Must lie somewhere ahead.
On the long train journey through France
We slept on luggage racks,
Gossiped, scoffed spam sandwiches
And marvelled at poplar-lined roads
Through shabby villages rooted in the past.
We dozed and woke to find we had entered
A picture book, a country of lakes
And mountains, untouched by war.
The sun shone, the valleys were lush
While the mountains were still tipped with snow.
Old chalets dotted the green meadows and
We seemed to inhabit a fairy tale.
Cows, hung with deep-toned bells
Ambled past and on to higher pastures
Where we ate our picnics amidst the flowers.
Thick bread, filled with meat,
Hard boiled eggs, apples and cake.
Even the local boys seemed handsome
Gently flirting though separated by language.
There was nothing to spoil the memory
Of that rare and special week.
Yesterday, I bought a bar of Lindt chocolate.
As I peeled back that same mauve wrapper,
I was back in Stans, fifty-two years ago.

Ena Wordsworth

Countryside

The animals in the countryside
They roam around at ease
Now they have to cull them
Only because they did not heed
To the rules and regulations
Of other countries' foolishness
Where the standards are not met
So now we have to kill them
Even if they are your pets
When will this country learn
We are Britain and number one
Not to be fooled by politicians
And vets and soldiers' guns
The countryside looks awful now
No lambs frisking in the sun
Or cows chewing the cud
The land is bare
Just like when time begun
I love the countryside
The animals and the farms
Why should the farmers suffer
They never did any harm
If our land gets back to clean
And everything is happy and green
To keep our animals is I trust
Inspect the 'imports' is a must
My heartfelt sorrow for times like these
Maybe one day this country
Will be free of infection and disease

Jean Broadhurst

My Life

A year today life came to change,
My life to forever rearrange.
A piece of paper to explain to me,
My birth, my parents, my family.
After months of waiting this paper sought,
A nervous feeling with it brought.
Before I lived all alone,
Now the news to me it shown.
How the tears came to my eyes,
Among the relieving sobs and cries.
My given name revealed to me,
The names of parents for to see.
To turn the page the answers clear,
Now my kin to hold dear.
The number six penned in ink,
Two gone past, four left I think?
Now the need for me to find,
Answers remain to complete this line.
To seek the answers to ease my mind,
My life on paper came today . . .

Russell Bassett Stanley

The First Time That I Saw Her

The first time that I saw her,
   I'd swear my heart stood still,

To see her gentle loveliness
   gave me a special thrill,

Her limpid eyes of azure blue,
   the dimples in her cheeks,

No man could find a fairer,
   no matter where he seeks,

Her hair is made of silken thread,
   the colour purest gold,

And there's no doubt about it,
   my heart she'll always hold,

The first time that I saw her
   was the day that she was born

And what a joyous day it was
   on that November morn;

No wonder that I love her so,
   as you will clearly see,

When I tell you I'm her grandad
   and now she's nearly three.

   Brian Hope Gent

Fruit Stand

Standing out of the rain
Out of the crowd
By the fruit stand
Standing with the gooseberries
Still edgy
Still in the fog
Of troubled dreams

Standing, suitcase in my hand
I handle a melon
For the first time
She wasn't there last night
Not the way I needed
Not in the flesh
This fruit isn't really ripe

She steps out of the crowd
Into my world
We talk
She makes things clear
She says it's complicated
She says she's not coming back
She says I am not coming with her

A dream man
Walked into her life
She glances at the bananas
She takes the melon from my hand
She explains how much she hates
Long goodbyes
She leaves

I'm left
Standing with the nuts
She knows I'm watching her walk
Out of my life
Into the fog

Jason Donald

Lullaby For My Love

Sleep little one
For in my arms you are safe
You saved me
Sleep sweet one
Gain the peace you crave
I'll watch over you
Sleep small star
No harm will ever reach you
In my cradle-arms
Sleep dear heart
Sleep sound
My first, only love
My strength
My heart
My own
My daughter

Katie Commons

Dear Gran

Watery blue eyes 'neath heavy hooded lids,
A perfect nose above two perfect lips,
Silvery grey hair tops a wrinkled brow,
This was the face whose love was to show
The true meaning of the word,
Although with a tongue that could cut like a sword,
This was the love of my dear old gran.

This was my first love, the one that to me
Radiated its warmth for the whole world to see.
Of course, at this time when I was only four
I never knew what would happen except I would grow:
Then along came Kathleen, the girl next door
With eyes so rich they made me feel poor,
But hers weren't blue eyes, but hazel brown,
Shining twinkling, the best in town,
Until at last I met Marilyn, a homely girl,
A girl with a magical smile, and teeth like pearls.

Like my gran, her eyes are watery blue,
Perfect lips and now silver hair too,
Of course, this is the girl I took to be my wife
And a finer choice I could never again make in my life,
For now I am a grandad and Marilyn a gran herself,
And I know our grandchild will look back and tell,
How his gran was *his* first love, his true love as well.

F A Hoggarth

My First Flight

As I got on the plane,
I got a tummy pain,
It was hurting so much,
I had no lunch!
My brother played a trick,
I felt so very sick!
So guess what happened?

Holly McKeen (8)

First Job - 1942

First job
First day
Bank clerk
Low pay

> Make tea
> Buy buns
> Big queue
> Curse huns

Change date
Replenish ink
Wash pots
Tidy sink

> Counter set
> Ten o'clock
> Open door
> In they flock

On the go
In a whirl
At everyone's
Beck and call

> Close door
> Half past three
> Once again
> Make tea

Five o'clock
Accounts done
Cash checked
Off home

> Working girl
> First job
> First pay
> Fifteen bob

Vera Watson

Softly, So Softly First Love

Softly so softly I whisper your name
I'd cradle you in my embrace,
Stroke your dear face,
Plant butterfly kisses on your eyes
That look with love into mine,
Hold you my dear through all the years
We'd journey into a world apart
Our world alone, sweetheart,
See first the magic of your smile
Let's linger a little while,
Taste the sweetness of your lips
The warmth of each kiss,
While time stands still
We'll wander at will
Hand in hand in our magic land
In our country of love
Our own heaven on earth
The sweet land that lovers know
Where only the cream of love flows
Spellbound I'm held enchanted by you
Invisible threads hold me enthralled
The web of love, stronger than any chains
Softly, softly I whisper your name
Sunbeams dance in tune with my heart
What wonderful dreams when fantasy wings
Her capricious way, oh wonderful day,
Dreams that tantalise and tease,
Floating on clouds fluffy and light
Bewitched, breathless with delight
I hold you, love you, through the night

Gently, hasten not my love
We're together in our country of love
Where the sun shines bright all the time
Because you are mine
The air is perfumed and rare
In this dream of eternal delight
With you through the night
Softly, so softly I whisper your name.

J Nolan

Ice-Skating

As I slither on the ice
I'd rather dance through fire.
The mist is numbing my ankles,
So I raise my thoughts higher
To the harshness of the music
That howls above the rink.
I'm balancing on delicate blades
And panicking too much to think.
My fingers claw at the handrail,
Lest I tumble to the coldness below.
I trust my more confident friends -
But only so far as I can throw.
Racers flash past, soppy dancers twirl,
But I'm wobbling on one spot,
Forbidding painful risks to unfurl.
I know there is no way to stop
Unless you try hurtling at the wall,
And my blue fingers will be guillotined
If I allow myself to fall.
My friends ask if I'm having fun.
I tell them exactly what I think,
But unfortunately loud enough for all to hear:

'Get me off this stupid ice rink!'

Angela Cullen

My First Love

First I saw you in the doorway
Then you sauntered into the room
You were top to toe in leather
My heart went boom boom boom

Be still my beating heart I thought
As your eyes they held my gaze
Deep in my heart I thought I knew
With you I'd end my days

At first we got on really well
But then the bubble burst
I tried you tried we tried
But it went from bad to worse

So once more you're standing in the doorway
But your eyes don't hold my gaze
After talking rowing and crying
We're going our separate ways.

Gillian Morphy

My First Day In London

My vision was blocked,
People rushing around some heading for the underground,
Some heading towards business places with briefcases.

We went to the British Museum,
And saw the magnificent Rosetta Stone,
Beautifully carved in hieroglyphics,
Set in the darkness of marble,
The mummies were wrapped in cage after cage.

Pigeons in Trafalgar Square,
They are spread out everywhere,
Pigeons gliding in the air swoop and sway on a windy day.

Tanisha Croad (10)

My Firstborn ~ Steven

Laying in my hospital bed
My baby born, both exhausted
I heard a whisper, 'Is her baby dead?'
The realisation hit of what was said.

Fear gripped me laying there at night
A nurse enquired, 'Are you all right?'
I explained; she saw my plight
Assuring me he was well and bright.

Apart from him for seven days
Because of flu my mind was all a-daze.
Recovered well, they let me stay
To hold his hand through this phase.

A real fighter he proved to be
This tiny person held for all to see,
And with the sunlight shining through the trees
From the hospital we were at last home free.

Margaret Smith

My First Love

I dreamt of you so very much
When we held hands, with a Heavenly touch
I dreamt of you, as if it was yesterday
When we held each other, in a romantic way

So many regrets, I knew within my heart
The way I failed, and we did depart
Yet, within a foolish heart, I cry
Wondering, if you are inland or in Heaven high

So innocent, yet so very young
When we were teenager, you were strong
You loved me, as I loved you so
My very first love, of long ago.

I still vision you, in your uniform
A man so tall, such a vision in form
Just like it was only yesterday
Oh, sweet love, why did we stray

A man so upright, through his stride
A guardsman, yet without any pride
Oh, my first love, of the past
I dream of you, till the last

Jean P Edwards McGovern

All Worthwhile

The flats we live in are close to the city,
We are very content, and we said, 'What a pity,
A garden is what these flats lack,
Made from wasteland out the back.'
A whisper went round, the pipeline hummed,
We were to get a garden from a concealed fund.
We waited - it seemed never-ending this wait,
The whisper perhaps was only a bait.
But at last, things began to happen very fast,
Men with spades and drills loud blast,
Worked very hard and slogged all day,
No one had anything much to say.
The garden took shape under hammer and pick,
And before our eyes formation came quick.
Now with plants and flowers and privacy at last,
All grouses and grumbles a thing of the past.
The wonders of nature will unfold next year,
Giving joy and pleasure to all that live here.
To those whose 'fingers were in the pie',
We thank you all, with a heartfelt sigh.

Beatrice Newman

First Light

It was then that poetry
Caught up with me
On Pablo Neruda's street
Sticking to thirty
Hard by the clink
The man stone ahead
The woman solicitous
Arm crooked around
Her man's night in
Custody

Liz Statham

The First Visitors To Namuh Dnik

It happened only a while ago, when space was still exotic, to all but
just, a fleetly chosen crew.

There had been a drafting, to see who had lost the chance, and some
ordained, to conscript, an optimistic vision.

It wasn't that they wanted, to be the first to go, nor did a sense of
hazard, inspire, their doomy fate.

All heralded a new accord; was called, 'The Century of Love' seeking
peace and promise, in universal view.

Then journeyed they with covenant and looked upon the starry black,
seeking secret haven, of friendship and admission.

They searched throughout the heavens, plunderous war and struggle
raged, nowhere loving flourished; all was steeped in hate.

The Universe was rummaged and searched were another two, each
planet was excluded, as onwards went the test.

Long past the robust moonbeams, of a tardy dying light, thence the
twinless mountains, of unhuman pedigree.

Beyond a blessed circle, of fire-set cratered, stones and on to where
the cauldron of the past, was maiden lit.

Fore long there came a planet, that woke this chosen few, and much
was made, of hoping; an end to earthly quest.

'Twas studied for a minute; soon gave up its name, they tried then
very godly, a secret to set free.

At last, was made resolve to, enter Namuh Dnik and taking every
prudence, to berth and be admit.

Set down then in sheepfold, first saw a little maid, who told them of a
visioned and, kindly mother seen.

Showing not a jot of interest, in this hovelled peasant croft; visions
unimportant, to questing great for peace.

Then journeyed them some distance, to an unfamiliar scape, saw hint
of copious, upset and ruin on the wheat.

At last they came across a flattening, vast in its expanse, full of turbid
trenches and a smell of human sheen.

It was chiefly boneyard and shrapnel deadly lay, next to bullet
tattered banners, of aims in great decease.

Grasped closely by a grey corpse, which had seen some better times, a
catechism was clasped, in the anger of defeat.

The leader of the Peacefuls, first to have a look, saw the words in vain
it shouted, as its pages quietly bled.
The title was no secret
And soon the heroes read,
'First kill the unbelievers until,
their souls are,
dead'.

Francis McDermott

First Love

When you were but an infant
I cradled you in my arms,
Sheltered from harm, sang you songs.

When you were a tiny boy
I dried your tears, chased your fears,
Patched your cuts, eased painful ears.

Time passed a young man at last.
I was mother confessor,
Champion and protector.

All too soon the bird had flown
Itching to stand all alone,
In a world I'd never known.

Now you're a man my son
Days of freedom long gone.
With a family of your own.

In silence I watch and weep.
To solve your problems I'd seek,
But my counsel now I keep.

Kathleen Potter

My First Acceptance

My first poem accepted
The joy of not being rejected

Acceptance makes up for the piles of paper thrown on the floor
I hear my children ask 'Dad, why is Mum
Again behind the locked door'

Hours of writing not now written in vain
To me this is an honourable gain

There for all my family to have a look
Mum's proof of a poem printed in a poetry book

M Wood

Kites (My First Poem)
(Dedicated to my mum)

Kites are flying everywhere,
Some near the ground, some in the air.
Soaring high in the sky, carried by the breeze,
Up, up and away far above the trees.

Kites swoop and dive like birds on the wing,
The children pulling and guiding the string.
Kites twist and twirl, their tails curling,
The wind is blowing, whistling and whirling.

A cry of help comes from the ground,
A little boy turning and turning around.
Struggling and pulling with all his might,
Up, up and away, he's now with his kite.

Suzanne Shepherd

Kelsea

(Dedicated to my granddaughter, Kelsea)

Major surgery the doctors had to perform
For my first grandchild to be born,
You see my daughter was very ill
Couldn't be fixed with medicine or pill,
Nine-thirty-three a.m. I heard her first cry
Big brown eyes not blue like the sky.
Her little head full of hair
Not bald, but dark, no not fair,
In an incubator she had to go
Six weeks too early she had to grow,
Fifteenth of December, in this world she came
Falling in love with her no one could blame,
A tiny bundle, all of four pounds nine
My daughter cried is she really mine.
I turned and kissed her tears away,
Then I thanked the doctors for their help today.
Four months now have passed on by
Since little Kelsea gave her first cry,
Each day she greets us with a smile so fine
This little precious granddaughter of mine.

Sylvia Mudford

Starting School

Mum's calling me to get up
as I start school today,
I'd rather stay at home
so I can go and play.
She makes me eat my breakfast
though my stomach's on the churn,
she says you've got to go to school
or else you'll never learn!
I have to wash behind my ears
and my hair it must be smart,
then I put on my uniform
I hate that for a start.
I feel like my old grandad
in a shirt and tie,
then my dad goes and says to me
as he is passing by
you look a 'bobby-dazzler'!
As I am smartly dressed
I thought he said 'bobbly-duster'
so I wasn't that impressed.
When I get up tomorrow
I've now made up my mind,
the rest of you can go to school,
'but me' I'll stay behind.

Neata Todd

My First Love

When I was a girl of just sixteen
I met a young boy of my dreams
On our bikes we'd go for rides
Laughing happily side by side
Then we'd find a secluded place
Where he gently kissed my face
He carved our names upon a tree
Somewhere no one else could see
Then somehow we grew apart
So I said goodbye to my young sweetheart
There were others in between
But nothing to me did they mean
I looked around as time went by
Another young man caught my eye
At the local Palais de Danse
There I met him just by chance
Fresh faced features and strong chin
I could not take my eyes off him
We danced around both fast and slow
'Til it came time for us to go
He led me back across the floor
And asked if he could walk me to my door
With my heart beating fast
Hoping this time love would last

Doris Lilian Critchley

Memory

How came it to me,
This clear and lucent memory
Of a moment past,
The feeling not forgotten
Yet flitted from my grasp.

How came I to life
And life to me,
A single soul-spun mystery.

Lisa J Kilty

Txt Msging

the 1st txt msge i sent
didnt mke much sense
but i didnt wont 2 shout
abuv the din of mobile bleeps
but now ive got the hang
of this txt msging slang
i can tell my grlfrnd
that i luv u
evry day xxx

Mark Follows

Sheila

My first love, my mother's there,
  Looking into her gentle eyes,
She gave me love with tender care
  And always listened to my cries.

Sheila as always, my mother dear,
  Loving memories will always last,
Even though you are no longer here
  And your days have sadly passed.

Mother you live on in all I do,
  Each and every day,
Sheila dear, I do love you,
  With all my heart I pray.

  Andrew Perrins

The First Time . . .

The first time I held your hand
I felt a friend indeed
Little did I know that
You'd become a friend in need

The second time I held your hand
I felt a stir within
Little did I know that
You'd become a game to win

And so it was as hand in hand
We'd pass the many days
Togetherness as if but one
The first and lasting ways

Lin Bourne

My First Grandchild

Three weeks before the birth
I visit; and just for once,
she lets me help.

Now conscious of her girth,
at eventide she swims:
and lets me cook.

And, coming down to earth,
the garden bristling weeds,
she lets me dig.

Then recognising worth
- enticing gap to fill -
she lets me saw.

And soon, mummied in milk,
sweet shawls and love's caress,
she'll let me hold.

Harold Wonham

New Life

At the home it was plain to see
This little chap had a smile for me
From head to toe I surveyed his form
Bright blue eyes and soft blonde hair
Here he was for us to care.

His skin was smooth and felt like silk
He smelt so clean with a hint of milk
My thumb was gripped oh so tight
He showed his will for life that night
There he was for us to care.

His mum was pleased to see
This little bundle of energy
Out of the darkness and into the light
Thankful that everything was alright
There he was for us to share
To show him love and devoted care.

Richard Phillips

Bitterne Park (Remembering That First Kiss)

They've vanished now those fields of waving corn,
Forever gone the little dancing stream;
Tall trees which gave us shade are but a dream -
Our laughing youth can never be re-born -
Its banner in the wind of time lies torn.
Now ribbon roads and houses are the scene
Where golden gorse once caught the radiant glean
Of sunlight cradled in eternal morn.
No longer stands the stile where first we kissed
When moonlight sent her magic over fields
Of scented clover - age now gently yields
Itself to mem'ries gath'ring in its mist

Where once we dreamed and loved and sang youth's song
The hand of progress scars its mark along!

John Paget

A First To Remember

Yesterday we went off to explore
Just Martyn and me - he's only four
Our first expedition as man and boy
A big new world for us to enjoy.
We started off all tidy and neat
But muddied ourselves down the path to the beach,
We skimmed flat stones across the mirror surface of the sea
And watched ripples merge and disappear to infinity.
He found a poor bird washed up on the shore
'Is he dead, Grandad, - he's not breathing no more?
How did he die, - do you think he drowned?'
'Probably,' I mused, with a knowing frown.
So we dug a big pit with our own bare hands
And laid Sammy Seagull to rest in the sand.
We befriended a big black dog and threw him a stick
He splashed in the sea - retrieved it ever so quick
Just stood there staring, with hypnotic power
Violently shook himself and gave us a shower.
The sun shone and soon we were dry,
But we didn't give Blackie another try!
We drew a big face where the sand was wet,
Lots of slimy seaweed for hair we fetched
Pebbles for the eyes, a limpet for the nose
Small pearly shells for teeth we carefully chose.
A huge wave came and washed him all away
Ah! Great sadness, shock, horror, such dismay.
So off we went to find the secret gypsy camp
Peeped in a window - see the big brass lamps.
Jumped on a swing held by a fraying rope
'Could you catch me Grandad if it broke?'
And soon it was time to be on our way
Sorry old chap - but we'll do it again another day.

M J Elliott

To Be True To Us

I have been commissioned by my soul
To at least let you for all time to know
That in all truth and love I have to let you go
It said to me could you not see
That what you made is now

With love and dreams then wishes true
We built a beautiful woman just for you
To watch as a guardian of angels three
A perfect place, a position to be
The truth I told to you long days ago

That to drift away when I had made you so
This was prime directive one
There in the sky were two suns
That touched their souls on passing by
The touch that caused even the angels to cry

It was told that in this fleeting times
Each sun held the other, so deep in mind
They stood there still, as was their destiny
They swapped their love and stored the energy
For all times held just you and me

Now that their journey has again begun
Is held of each, in the soul of each one
The distance now as they have to fly
Grows greater in their own velvet sky
The changes made of their touching days

Eternally held as they wend their ways
To meet one day, as all matter must come
There in eternity to shine as one sun
Eternally

Yenti

78

First Kiss

Mouths barred and bolted
Become luscious lips, parting
Touching tender feelings
In a supple, soft smooch

Inhaled breath held in one
Being exhaled into another
Ending innocence, awakening
Deeper intimacy

Disturbing yet thrilling
The heart's easy pulse until
Wet and tongue tied, tameless
Desire wakes a music

Ah, but the soul's memory is long
To remember lips kissing
For the first time, unleashing
Unfulfilled fanciful fantasy

Mary Cathleen Brown

First Flight

We're going down the runway,
And travelling much too fast,
My stomach's in my armpits,
And my life is flashing past.

There's a very strange sensation,
Coursing through my blood,
And no, it's not the alcohol,
Though a drink sounds pretty good.

I'm sucking on my boiled sweet,
As if it were my last,
My life is in the hands of fate,
The final die is cast.

We're lifting now into the air,
Of fear there is no lack,
But even if I do survive,
It's the thought of getting back.

Helen M Jones

My Alan, My Love

My Alan stands tall
among the crowds
of grey men outshone.
Igneous rock towering
over shards of dull shale,
the breakwater holds
as the soft stones slide.

This strong, gentle man
shields our hearts from pretenders;
he is my refuge from the world
and I live him.

Elizabeth A Pepper

A First Worth Waiting For

When I was just a school girl how I longed to be
First at maths or English (or even geography)
The teachers used to say to me 'Please will you pay attention'
But I was dreaming of the day I'd come first with my 'invention'
If, just once the teacher said, 'You are first to me'
But I soon learned the hard way, (that this was not to be)
So many 'firsts' throughout one's life, so many to recall
But hearing my daughters call me 'Mum'
Was my most precious 'first' of all.

Janice Smith

First Love

Bid her live, her life to give
And I her love will earn
Sick she is, no will to live
That I, her lover, can discern.

Her heart is soft, her heart is kind
And I for love am pining
Weak she is, no strength she'll find
That I might say she's willing.

Cold she is, her limbs are cold
And I for her can feel a chill
Down to my marrow bold,
I her lover still.

Fear in her eyes, her eyes are dark
Their darkness I can see
Where two round orbs stark
Are pointing straight at me.

Her looks are floating, floating her looks
I see them dark with tragedy
On a tide, her eyes a rook's
Outstaring life's set comedy.

Away she went, she went away
And I am left with nothing,
Nothing save a memory grey
And a heart still longing.

Angus Richmond

My First Teddy Bear

He was no Winnie the Pooh, but I loved that old bear.
He was round and grey with a little white muzzle.
Red thread held his tummy together and
he had a patch on his arm. His coat had lost
its softness and felt like old wool. He always smelt
of calamine lotion after I had chicken pox.
One ear would hang half off
from when I used his hat as a fruit bowl.
When he sat his head flopped to the left.
He was great to dress up and to have tea with.
When I got older I would hide things
in the gaps in his stitching. He was great
to tell my secrets too, and would always be there
when I needed a cuddle. He soon emigrated
to a cupboard, but sometimes I allow him out,
for an airing.

Linda M Adams

My First Grandson

A dear little boy came into my life
Several years ago,
How I existed before he came
I really do not know.
With steel blue eyes and soft fair hair
A beautiful baby was he,
And nothing was nicer than cuddling him close,
Or sitting him on my knee.
Soon babe to toddler quickly turned,
Face, scarlet with rage,
'Til I gave him my attention
And read stories, page by page.
Soon he became a little man
Dressed in school attire,
We'd go for walks and find some swings,
'Push me Nana- higher.'
But then as he grew older,
Didn't need me quite the same,
Though I sometimes came in handy
For joining in a game.
But all too soon those years have gone,
He's almost in his teens,
But I'll still be there to help him,
Fulfil his hopes and dreams.

Margaret Whitton

Evolved, Or Devolved?

Did we crawl from the sea
to set foot on the moon?
We've sent ships that view us from the stars.
Back to earth, vision's clouded;
we've felt red dust from Mars,
will our zenith slip through coarsened hands?

Or were we placed here
with an urge to explore?
Did we seize power or is it a loan?
Gifted, touched from above,
should we look into our souls
or learn why we're here from afar?

Are we animals yet?
Evolved beyond control,
crippled, scarred by our struggles to live.
Or tantalised tenants,
blessed, or cursed, with a choice,
obliged to improve then pass on?

Ian Newman

My First Poem

I wish I had a little boat
To sail upon the sea
If I had that little boat
I truly would be free

Alas I have no little boat
To sail upon the sea
So of all the things that I desire
Freedom eludes me

R P Walker

First Love

We have only done
What thousands of years ago
Other lovers did too.
They lay beneath the sun,
Watching the endless curve of sky,
The slender tops of leafy trees,
The green against the blue.
They knew their love would never wane,
But stay as fresh as summer rain,
Fragrant, sweet and true.

And did they,
Suddenly turning to each other,
Feel as we did today?
So awed by the strength of passions unfurled,
That nobody mattered in all the world,
Except me - and you.
And when your lips met mine in bliss,
Did they think too?
We are the first, the *very* first,
To love as perfectly as this.

Margaret Lewis

My First . . . Best Friend

This poem is for two Emmas
Who are my best friends
And with them I hope
Our friendship never ends

My first best friend was Emma
Who I met at birth
We played together all the time
We shared nearly everything.

Then at three
I met another Emma
When I went to nursery
She also became a best friend

Lucy Adams (10)

First Class

When first we found that you were due
It came as quite a shock,
For we had thought that it was wind,
Until Mum saw the Doc.
Expectations.

And ever since, through your growing years,
We've often had to stop,
And think that, once again, your tricks
Had caught us on the hop.
Frustrations.

But still, through all the twists and turns,
We've seen your other side,
The things you've done that made us smile,
And filled our hearts with pride.
Aspirations.

So of course we were not surprised,
We knew you'd pass the test,
That you would surely graduate,
Cos our girl is the best.
Congratulations.

Brian Hartley

Memories

And as I sit
Memories cascade my mind
Fallen forgotten memories
Oh, to live that summer again
When my mind was kissed
By your gentle embrace
And fears were a thing of the past
Your warmth caressed like that of the sun
And your kiss would ease the pain
Please return to me the same
Don't change within the chains of time
But remain as fresh as the flower
That I held when we first met.

C F Ballard

First Solo

The instructor said, as he walked away, 'Right! Now you're on
your own,
Off you go' and I fought the panic, as I'd never flown alone;
I saw as he strode towards the club, that he didn't even look round;
'That's all he cares' I thought, now he's safely back on the ground.

My heart was thumping though I knew my spirits were soaring high
For this is what I'd always wanted, I'd always longed to fly.
Going through all my cockpit checks till at last I felt quite calm
Except for the quicker heartbeat and the sweating in each palm.

With the throttle slowly opening, the 'Tiger' forward crept,
My confidence was rising as my eyes on the dials I kept.
Feeling the tail now lifting, and the aircraft wanting to fly,
The instructor's words rang in my ears, 'Keep watch on your ASI.'

The wheels at last stopped trundling, and the 'Tiger' floated free,
And slowly climbing skyward, I thought, 'Is this really me?'
Now levelling off, I realised just what 'true happiness' meant,
The wind sang in the flying wires, the 'Gipsy' purred content.

Eyes searched the sky for other craft as I slowly turned the plane,
Two circuits were all I had to do before setting down again.
With throttle closed, and gliding down, but remembering to heed
The instructor's words 'Watch your ASI and remember your
stalling speed.'

Then came 'touch-down' stick easing level, we rumbled to a halt;
I offered up a thankful prayer for a landing without fault.
The instructor then came forward, saying, 'Good show, this
calls I think
To visit the bar and you can buy *me* a very much needed drink . . .'

Alf Godman

92

That Night

To look back and remember that night
The night I wanted to be mine
To be special
The night I dreamt would
Hypnotise me and change the rest of my
Life
The night I waited for and wanted to be ours
To look back and remember that night
That I had imagined would put me into a daze
That would leave my head spinning
That would leave me feeling like a real woman
Like someone special
The night I had fantasised about as
An extraordinary feeling felt between us
Magic
To look back and remember that night
That I had wanted so badly to amaze me
Ended up being just another night with a little
Extra something?
To look back and remember that night
To look back and remember what I wanted it to be
I wish that night had never happened in that way
I wish that night had never happened to me!

Katy Morley

My First Love

My first love
was the boy next door,
we children, played
in field and farm,
with brothers and our friends.
Oh! To watch our
school burn down,
half way, one day,
now 'holidays' a week
to win.
No classrooms to share
a crumbling mess.
Our childhood, fun and work
and games,
grown up, those teenage years,
music, homework, laughter, tears
not speaking as on buses
travel home again all is well.
To city and more learning
suddenly *a spark* alights
our puppy love is
oh so right.
Passion, wishing to be new
that was so from the start.
But later, parting of the ways
took place,
jobs and wartime people.
Broke the spell
so to end . . .
Romance has gone
and a broken heart
to mend.

Audrey Rogers

Kaylee

When I first saw your face
And held you in my arms,
I immediately fell
For your baby charms.

You gurgle and coo
And smell so fresh,
Except after a sleep,
When you've made a mess!

The world turns upside down
With one little being
A continuous round
Of feeding and cleaning.

But when you lay
In your cot at night,
I look and wonder
At such a small mite.

What in the world
Will you eventually be?
Whatever it is,
You're still precious to me.

Mary Graham

Memories

When Dorothy and I
Where 4 and 5 we went
To Sunday School
Miss Pratt and Miss Coles
Looked after us with other
Boys and girls

We marched around
Singing hear the pennies
Dropping listen how they
Fall every one for Jesus
He shall have them all

As we grew older
To the juniors we went
Then to the seniors we
Sang hymns, and chorus
And our Bible we read

Gladys Bartley

Michael My 1st Born Son

Michael my 1st born son
Born 19th August 2000
He is my angel millennium boy
My 1st child
My 1st little angel
Michael Apollo Ronan Chakotay Knight
My 1st born child
He is a delight, an angel, a treasure
My beautiful baby boy born August 2000
A millennium Leo boy
He will grow up to be a great man
He will grow up treasured and loved
My son Michael, my 1st born
He is my boy, he is all mine
My angel, my Michael, my little boy
My 1st born child
I will have more children
Michael Apollo Ronan Chakotay Knight
My 1st born angel boy
My little knight rider
My angel, my little boy
I love my son, Michael
Yes my 1st born

Michelle Knight

A First Magical Moment

The first time I saw fairies
Dancing in the dell
I was just a little child
Who was very far from well.

They looked delicate and airy
Translucent in the light,
More fragile than the butterflies
As they stood poised for flight.

They smiled at me and waved their wands
Which calmed me down somehow
Then they sent a puff of wind
To cool my fevered brow.

They touched my eyes with stardust
So I could fall asleep
But they didn't stay till I awoke
For my slumber was too deep.

Although I searched for many years
I never saw them again
But I remember clearly
How they took away my pain.

Sometimes I think I hear them laugh
When the air is very still
And imagine they are comforting
Another child who's ill.

Betty Nevell

My First
(Written after four miscarriages)

A first born, I long waited to greet
At times I thought we would never meet
Time and again I tried in vain
Hopes were dashed again and again
With empty arms and lonely days
With patience too, a virtue which pays
The years go by, then, 'oh the joy'
To know I have delivered a beautiful boy,
Nestling in my arms at last
To love and cherish till time is past
Safe in my arms, I hold him near,
Never was a baby loved so dear.

Kathleen Glover

My First Child

The day I found I was pregnant
I was filled with mixed emotions
Was I ready, could I cope
Will I be a good mother
How would I know if this little person,
Who depends on me for everything,
Would love me even if I made mistakes
That I wouldn't be blamed later in life
As the weeks flew by
I could feel the precious
Bundle begin to move inside
I was confident, I would be the
Best I could be to my baby
The day finally arrived
Excitement welled up inside me
I would get to hold my baby very soon
Well he kept us waiting nearly 30 hours
Before he decided to show
At the moment he was placed in my arms
My heart was bursting with pride
My first child, I love him so dearly
Forever in my heart and forever together

Samantha Vaughan

First Love

I had no thought he cared though we travelled every day
Monday through Friday to and from school
in a home-made box on wheels
euphemistically called 'The Bus'
Wartime no frills board seats canvas blinds
to pull down when it rained

We sang top ten hits to pass away the miles
hanging out the washing on the Siegfried Line
Seeing in our minds bluebirds flying over
white cliffs in England's Dover
Lilli Marlene waiting for her lover
in the lamplight near the barrack square

Thirty or so country kids whose only journey
ever was from Gladstone north through Laura
dropping off in ones and twos along the way
I don't remember where he came from
only that he left The Bus long after
those of us who lived in Laura disembarked

The day he shyly handed me
the block of Old Jamaica at a time
when chocolate was very hard to come by
brought a roar of ribald teasing from the boys
perched like birds along the back who saw
themselves a step or two ahead in worldly ways

I blushed not knowing how
one should respond to such attention
fixed my gaze on scenery and slipped
the treasure quickly in my school case
My heart warmed to him and the chocolate
like no other tasted then or since

He had red hair and freckles
we called him 'Marmaduke'
I think I never knew his proper name.

Betty Hocking

A First At Public Speaking

What can I do with my hands
And legs as wobbly as two rubber bands
I got to my feet and peered out at the faces
Then my poor heart started going to the races
I opened my mouth and out came a strange voice
It was mine as I began the talk of my choice
The time sped by and I was almost through
Would anyone really hiss or boo?
Expressions they say can tell a thousand words
With some smiling some blank one nodding
Off bringing in the herds
Good gracious it is all over and hands begin
To clap together I'm happy to say
My first speech in public and I've survived the day

Octavia Hornby

Over The Border

The very first time we set sight
on the place we had only dreamed,
we couldn't believe our eyes
just how unreal it seemed.

Over the border to Scotland
is where we wanted to go.
But mainly to the Highlands
where peaks are covered in snow.

From the dark and deepest lochs
where Nessie remains a mystery.
To the tallest of mountains
which are steeped in history.

The hauntingly beautiful Glencoe
is where the massacre took place
between the McDonalds and the Campbells
and where they came face to face.

An eerie sort of silence
which now envelops the glen,
leaves you with an experience
of wanting to go there again.

From the border of Scotland
to the remotest of parts,
the memory of the Highlands
will remain close to our hearts.

Pauline Russell

My First Glimpse Of A Snail Meeting

I went out in the garden when
The stars were sealed up in the sky
A nightly dew had damped the paths
And what a sight entranced my eye

For all the snails were mustering
To greet the dawning day
Grey ones, brown ones, banded and whorled
Came out to dance and play

All ages, sizes, shapes converged
Coming from hither and thither
And tiny babies, barely hatched
Were taking their first slither

Gardeners do not like them
Since they nibble plants that grow
But since I had that morning sight
I think of them, as a Buddist might
As my fellow-guests here below.

Elsie Karbacz

Our Love
(Dedicated to John)

You make me laugh
You make me cry,
But without you my love -
I would die.

To hear your voice
My heart gives a sigh of rejoice,
Just to see your face
I can feel my heart race.

I love you so much
Your sweet face I love to touch,
I place a kiss on your lips
And through your hair - I run my fingertips.

Our love is so very deep
You are always there, even as I sleep,
We know each other's minds
We also know - this love is hard to find.

   E R Bridgewater

The Golden Spring

Life's fabric is a strange and wondrous thing;
Its warp is happiness, its weft is sorrow,
And I could not foretell that lovely spring
That we would meet and love would quickly follow.

Young lips were smooth and sweet like mellowed wine,
Whose vintage even Bacchus would applaud,
And grapes of gladness, ripened on the vine,
Distilled fermenting hearts with true accord.

Affection's links were forged by soft words spoken;
No Gordian knot could match its powerful chain.
Such lasting bonds, once tied, could not be broken,
For memories of rapture will remain.

Time reaps the harvest of our golden spring,
Then stores its joys to make our senses sing.

Celia G Thomas

My First Poem

Do I remember still? Yes, I was seven.
The teacher told the class, 'Each one
must write a poem.' I can recall my pen,
its metal nib; the ink which slowly ran
staining my small and very busy hand;
and blue blob, that spreading, fell
on the wooden desk from the inkstand.

Thus it began: from a few words I chose
to come to life on paper yellow-white
I sifted meanings, felt their sound and rose
to heights unknown yet to a child. Tonight,
so many years from that first joyful time
when I perceived my song hidden inside,
finds me here still, to sing by words and rhyme.

Daniela Lampariello Taylor

In Love

Have you ever been in love?
Really and truly in love?
I don't mean in love with someone
Or something.
Have you ever been *in* love?
I mean have you ever felt
As if you were surrounded *in* love
Right up to your ears and higher
So deep *in* love that you *feel* loved.
It happened to me for the first time
When I was sitting on a fallen tree
In the middle of a little wood.
I closed my eyes and immediately
I saw the most beautiful pink colour
Behind my eyelids.
Then it started, the feeling.
From my toes
Moving right up to my heart.
Tears spilled over my cheeks and down my neck.
It continued on up till I was completely immersed.
I felt love, just for me!
As I write this an echo of the moment returns.
I believe that we are all *in* love
If I had one wish.
I would wish for each and everyone of you to *feel* it.

Dolly Little

My Solo

They say you're never too old, new things to do.
For me in my life, that certainly has proved true.
I've always loved to sing, bursting into song.
Out shopping, at work, and walking along.

When working my boss would worried be -
If I wasn't singing - had she upset me.
Never thought, that my voice was good, or strong.
Just enjoyed it, any chance for a singalong.

When at church a group was asked to lead the praise.
Was quite happy to join them, my own voice to raise.
Then my friend's mother died, two years ago,
It was Christmas time, her mother's favourite carol she did know.

Felt it would be good at the funeral, for someone to sing.
Would I do it? she asked, when she did me ring.
'You're joking,' I laughed nearly dropping the phone,
No I'm not, you'd be great, singing on your own.

In 'the bleak midwinter', the carol of mum's choice
At a funeral service, the first time to use my solo voice.
No it's never too late, to undertake things new,
I was nearly seventy, when this first solo I did do.
Since then, I've been asked to sing quite a few.
As well as leading singalongs, which I often do.

E Griffin

Return To Innocence

The warmth, the safety of strong arms
A childhood innocence embalms
The walks we took, my hand in his
There was no play to equal this
Strong like an ox, of sturdy frame
How silently he played the game
A man of few words, full of love
And like a giant he towered above
The hand encompassed in his own
Would never feel it had outgrown
This haven of paternity

Phillippa Benson

A Country Man's First Signs
Of Spring And Summer

Cold wet days of winter have gone at last,
Now the mad march hares go dashing past,
Time has come to look at the larch and pine,
Those beautiful red flowers growing so fine,
To turn into a little green fir cone this will grow,
Then it will hang on the tree a perfect show,
Singing of the frogs coming from the pond,
Tadpoles will still grow if the water pongs,
Little carpets of primroses trying hard to hide,
With beautiful yellow petals open very wide,
Yellow catkins from the nut trees swing,
With the pussy willow trying to be its twin,
Under the tall trees bluebells thickly grow,
Sunbeams and shadows dancing making a show,
Young rooks climb out of nest upon a branch,
Flapping their wings doing a rock and roll dance,
Young rabbits along the hedgerows at play,
Hedgerows are gone they have taken them away,
Ditches have been filled in the old men had dug,
When it rains hard now the fields are in flood,
To find its own way out down the road it goes,
Filling roads and houses everywhere it flows,
On the river coots and moorhens they do dive,
Those beautiful white swans see them glide,
Swaying of the green corn in a gentle breeze,
Looking like the waves upon the seas,
New mown grass in the meadows do lay,
Waiting to be turned into sweet smelling hay.

Len Paget

Kiddie Car

I don't remember when my days had become so dreary;
going to and from the office feeling old, and weak, and weary.
While somewhere far away, like ghosts living in my mind
are memories of a childhood I vaguely think was mine.

But then again it couldn't be, I could never have been so small;
I've always had this lousy job, paid bills and been this tall.
Up by five every morning and out the door by seven
thinking of my paycheck as the best thing to heaven.

Still, I see in misty dreams days of sun and laughter
when I believed in fairy tales, and happily ever after.
Passing by a toy store, I remember wishing on a star
for a Fire Truck Deluxe, by Murray Kiddie Car.

It had hooks and ladders for fighting any blaze
and a handy steering wheel that could navigate a maze!
I hopped in and peddled fast while blowing on a whistle
pretending to cut through traffic like a lethal guided missile!

In my ever-ready, do or die, Kiddie Car of speedy red
I knew I looked so cool the chicks would all fall dead.
Mom was pretty mad when she heard what I had to say,
but then I simply stated, 'Dad says that every day!'

When she went after pop I was left with my crimson joy -
now that I had a car I was a man and not a boy!
I went tearing through the house, leaving squeaks and squeals,
but you know I never got a babe to go riding in those wheels . . .

That was so long ago it must have been someone else's life
because it seems I've always had a mortgage, kids, and wife.
But I remember no engine's speed ever matched that truck's;
how on earth could I forget my Kiddie Car Deluxe.

David E Nettles

My First Day
(as a student nurse - August 1940)

'6.30 Nurse, and time to rise' - Well, that could not be me -
Three weeks ago I was at school - 'Nurse' How could it be?

Then I spied the uniform, and leaped up from my bed -
Struggled with collar, cuffs, and cap which kept slipping from my
head!

Breakfast, then up the ward - it seemed so full of beds
All occupied and to be changed - '*Observe* the corners,' Staff Nurse
said.

Blackout boards on windows all had to be released;
And daylight flooded in the ward, and brought a sense of peace.

Bedpan round - 'Do carry six, you do *not* have all day -
There's folk to wash, and meals to serve: Now, carry them away.'

That seemed so simple - but that task exerted all my skill;
For those six once-empty bedpans were now liable to spill!

This day was operations day. We never had a minute,
As back and forth the trolleys went with patients without limit.

The aftercare was special for these patients 'coming round
From chloroform or ether' - observations were profound.

The only bomb to hit the town fell the night that I arrived.
The only casualty was in our ward; sadly, she did not survive.

The day seemed everlasting; there was so much to do;
Sweeping, dusting, answering phones; many tasks were new.

At last the day was over and we could dim the lights,
Blackouts boards were fastened; the ward a peaceful sight.

That first day's lost in history; it was a time of war.
For the day that I've remembered was sixty years ago.

   Mora Maish

First Love

We met one day in early spring,
I saw the sunlight touch your hair,
The gleaming reflections most everywhere.
I saw your shapely form so proud,
Which stood out among the crowd.
The startling colour of your eyes,
That show the love within that lies.
Those shapely lips of a delicate pink,
That skin so soft and smooth as silk,
To stir my mind and make me think.
What a beautiful lady that you are.
We stood and talked for quite a while,
What is this sensation that I feel.
Is this a dream or is it real?
This racing heart that seems so loud.
This feeling never felt before,
Like floating on a velvet cloud.
As light in mind you walk away,
And wake up on another day.
To find the feeling still fills your mind,
Then you realise that you are in love.

Thomas Usher

Upon First Discovering Fire

We all felt it from the earth,
But me and the tall one first discovered fire;
Others made claims, but we were first,
First ever into the gully.

We'd all circled South, and truly,
They were all feeling close -
But me and him slowed, got talking new ideas.
And that darkness flowed through us.

We decided to turn back,
And left them far, far behind
Believing though, all believing;
And it threw itself as the bird throws itself,
The small heart rapidly beating.

Each flame a pulse escaping the night,
Never seen so wild. Until then we never smiled.
We watched the site, served the world,
Until they discovered us the first time.
We stayed. They stayed. Too scared to leave:
And now fire stays with us.

S J Carter

My First Death

He had been deteriorating for some time,
Having been born with Downe's Syndrome,
Then getting Alzheimer's Amentia;
The end was inevitable.

Nursing had become difficult,
Emotionally as we watched helplessly
The loss of his personality and other faculties;
And physically as we struggled to get food and drink
Past his tongue and down his throat.

Clear fluids were all he could manage come the end,
While we watched and waited, doing the best we could
With tender loving care, and clear fluids.

The end came in the early morning, before we arrived for duty.
The night nurse showed me the body.
It was not horrible, or particularly peaceful, but like a waxwork
From Madame Tussaud's. Very white and waxy.

We could do nothing until the death had been certified.
In case of a mistake.
But there was no mistake. He was dead all right.
As I washed the body and put on the shroud, the reality hit home.
As I moved around the bed doing what was necessary, and he
                                        failed to respond,
I felt I should have prevented it. Never again would he sit up,
                                fidget or say 'Hello Darling,'
And, against all common sense, I felt personally responsible.

Some words from a poem we had read at school came flooding back;
'... It is no wonder her brown study astonishes us all ...'
And I understood what the poet meant.

Kathy Rawstron

117

My First Time

My first time? Now I remember.
It was an August or September,
In the evening after dark,
With a blonde girl in the park.
No, wait, there was one more,
When I was younger, long before.
A bad old man whom I slightly feared,
Not least because of his dirty beard,
Took me aside one afternoon
And told me it was not too soon.
He told me I was old enough
And said as I was big and tough
That I ought to open wide.
Then he put it deep inside,
I sucked a bit, then I swallowed.
A slightly nasty flavour followed
And it's been with me ever since,
From that first time I tried pepper-mints.

Peter Miles

First True Love

I've searched the whole world,
For my first true real love to be,
You wasn't available,
It wasn't meant to be me.

So many people have captured my heart and soul,
But you're the only one that makes me feel whole.
Your love and trust,
I will forever try to find,
Until that day when I finally make you mine.

A whole eternity I would give,
Your constant friendship strengthens my will to live.
Whenever I'm depressed, all I have to do,
Is close my weary eyes and think of you.

A vision from heaven,
That fell from the sky,
Defining beauty,
You make me so high.

That special sensation inside me,
Only you can convey,
Makes me weak at the knees,
And brightens my days.

I hope these feelings will never fade away,
As they keep my mind and heart at bay.
Words that creep out my mind,
With loving thoughts of you,
Because of that voice I find so divine.

Inside this mind, it tells me that you are the one,
My first vision of true love,
My number one.

David Wong

A New Venture

One day, fairly recently
I mentioned in a poem, the fact
That I must find something new
Upon which to act.

A few months have gone by
And I've had a great inspiration,
I've started a new venture
And it might cause a sensation.

I am what might be called
In the BBB
No, not the BBC! It's not an error,
It's the Boat Building Business, you see.

I don't think P & O Ferries need worry,
I won't set up in opposition,
For the very good reason, that
Mine will only be for exhibition.

You see it is only a model
And will only be twelve inches long;
Made up of hundreds of matches
Providing I don't do it wrong.

Other materials that I use, are
Glue, scissors, paint brush and tweezers,
Knife, card and block of wood,
And a guillotine for cutting the matches.

As I only work on it one day a week,
It will take several months to complete.
But, eventually this time will come,
Then I look for another new feat.

Judith Herrington

The First Little Flat

I remember quite clearly our first little flat
The first time we saw it said 'I want that'
We moved in at Christmas with just chairs of cane
And over the weeks new furniture came
We altered and painted, repaired and made good
And made it as nice as we possibly could

The kitchen was tiny and had cupboards none
Planning the new one was wonderful fun
We put in new heating, new windows and then
Oh joy! A new bathroom in fashionable green
Our half of the garden - nineteen feet by eight
Was divided from downstairs by a rickety gate

Oh those were the days - with energy high
With new ideas coming as each day went by
And after four years when it doubled its worth
We sold it and moved on a little way south
Over the years we've moved on a lot
But our first little home I never forgot

In the area recently we passed it by
I was shocked at the tatty and downtrodden way
The road now appeared when it had been quite smart
But the memory of our flat is within my heart
As I walked away sadly a young couple passed
The girl said 'Oh, darling our first home at last!'

I smiled as I heard those words once again
History repeating - then for us now for them
No doubt they will paint and repair and replace
The now dated decor with more modern taste
And I hope they enjoy the excitement to come
And remember with love as I do - my first home

Norma Griffiths

That Party

He stood aloof
Far from the throng
Tousled hair
Oversized sweater long
Spectacles dark-rimmed
Body fit, neat and trimmed.

A supercilious expression
Upon his face
'What am I doing here
I must escape'
Yet he danced with many
Of the leggy blondes
Showing vague interest
Yet his eyes fixed beyond.

My courage highlighted by
        the booze
I approached cautiously
He looked amused
We dance the night away
He came home, he stayed.

This man of mine
Sensitive, kindly, vague
Creator of music and lover
        of wine
Emotionally guarded but
        heart entwined with mine.

Ten years later we are as one
Still tousled hair, now grey
        and long
Together we belong.

   Gloria Hargreaves

My First Eclipse

I watched it all on the TV
Pictures from the Hercules, we see
How gradually the moon did bite
Into the sun obscuring light
Little by little, it ate it up
In just over an hour 'twas covered up
And we had totality
No sun at all were we able to see
Then the corona, fanning round
And a black darkness on the ground
Followed by the diamond ring
That was a fantastic thing
Next, a crescent reappeared
And, the darkness slowly cleared
Back to reality we came
And daylight was with us once again
A truly wonderful happening
Into our life it did bring
One that I'll remember long
Because the experience was so strong
What a great privilege to be
Able to watch, if only on TV
The spectacle was a delight to see
A wonderful sight for you and me

Joyce Metcalfe

(The First Time) I Saw John Wayne

Here was a man
Standing solid and proud
A tall rock of a man
Who stood out in a crowd.
Mainly in Westerns
He'd usually wear Stetsons
Carry rifle and pistols besides
Wearing jeans, boots and spurs
He may be trading in furs
And possibly peddling hides.

John could curse, drink and brawl
Regularly fight one and all
And do it with Hollywood style.
Whether shooting at Sioux
Or trying to woo
A wholesome young rancher's daughter
He'd know what to do and
You always knew he'd invariably do
What he knew he ought'a.

With his slow Midwest drawl
He'd welcome Y'all
And take you along for the ride.
Talking the talk
Walking his rolling walk
A great reason for American pride.
The first time I saw him on film
I had so much fun
I was his six year old sheriff
With a cap-popping toy gun.

Martin Hey

124

My Very First Poem

The first time I wrote
My very first rhyme
It came in a moment
All sweetness and light
My niece had a birthday
When out of the blue
I wrote her a poem
The paper was blue
A teenager she was about to become
The words were light hearted
She was over the moon
She took it to school
Showed her teacher the words
He read it out loudly
To the class, how absurd
She still has the poem
It's been thirty odd years
Now reads it she says
With a sigh and a tear

Jeanette Gaffney

Help

Can anybody hear me
Is there anybody there
Why won't anybody answer
Or don't you really care

I'm not wallowing in self pity
I'm quite a happy soul
I can usually just sail through life
I've just fallen in a hole

I need a friend, a help in hand
Someone to guide the way
I won't lean on you too harshly
Not like the others say

I've tried to sort things over
I've tried to work things out
I've tried to help myself along
Of that there is no doubt

Just give a minute of your time
And I'll be on my way
And I'll return the favour
Some dark and tearful day

Susan Olwen Papworth

Sympathy For Life

My first job was delivering the Christmas post,
An exploit about which I've never ceased to boast.
Three times a day, the last by the light of a torch,
For ten days we were in first this, then that strange porch.
Denis Holloway did the right side of the street,
I the left, that first time we realised we'd got feet.
When no one was in, I left mail with next-door folk,
Only to be warned once - *those* neighbours never spoke!
Wet, dry, rain, sun, ice, snow - varied weather was rife,
Ensuring all postmen my sympathy for life.

Allan Bula

My First Car

My first car was an old banger,
When I took out for a drive,
I knew I'd dropped a clanger.
The body was rusty,
And the tyres were worn,
The indicators did not work,
And I couldn't use the horn.
The engine had a cough,
And a tendency to seize.
The doors didn't fit properly,
In the winter I would freeze,
The steering had a wobble,
And wouldn't steer a straight line,
And from the gearbox,
Came an ear-shattering whine.
When it stopped completely,
And had run its last lap,
It fell apart completely,
I couldn't sell it,
It wasn't good enough for scrap.

F C Pelton

My First Love Was Donny Osmond!

I love you Donny! I would scream and shout,
And every article I would read about.
I heard how he made the other girls swoon,
And all his pictures lined my bedroom.
I would kiss every one before I went to bed at night,
To dream about my shining white knight.
Now I'm older and someone else has taken his place.
But Donny was my first love, that no one can replace.

Michelle Treacher

To My Granddaughter

I sit here recalling the years I have seen
'86 I remember, the best there has been.
December the thirtieth, on that special morn,
On that day, oh my darling, on that day you were born.

Remember the kissing tree, the old aeroport
Climbing the apple tree, a favourite sport,
Running to greet me one long summer's night
And the joy and excitement of your very first flight?

Grandee and Gran are the titles you chose,
And I and my lady are happy with those.
We both, as you know, think the world of you,
A few years ago the world thought so too.

They made you a champion for dancing prowess,
Trophy on trophy attest your success.
Starring in 'Grease' brought its own accolade,
Career foundations are now firmly laid.

From a babe to a youngster with long twirling curl,
I've watched you develop to a pretty young girl,
So bright, yet caprious, mischievous and kind,
Now lovely young lady with ambition defined.

But now comes another to steal your affection,
Now all of your glances are in his direction.
You're growing up fast, my sweet adolescent,
So lively and joyful, so effervescent.

Old head on young shoulder, it can never be,
Mistakes you will make - rely not on me.
Your life is a journey, you only can take
Yet as it progresses, many hearts you will break.

Come moments of pleasure, come moments of fears,
Occasions to treasure, occasions for tears.
When I am gone dear, I will still be here,
Death ever vanquished, life ever near.

The course of my life is almost run.
Yours, gentle creature has only begun.
So much to tell you, so much to impart,
Yet life is your tutor, my dear precious heart.

Maurice Bailey

School

When I first started I remember me saying
I don't want to go to school Mum, I'm happy playing
She took me up to the gates and waved me goodbye
Just like all the other kids I started to cry
I will be back said Mum to take you home
It was the first time my mum had left me alone
Well lessons started, I learnt two and two make four
But teacher told me I'd have to come back tomorrow to learn even more
All of a sudden a bell started to ring, and I heard teacher say
Time for your milk, to go out to play
We played marbles and conkers, hopskotch and all
Flicked fagg cards to see who could get nearest the wall
When the lessons finished and it was time to meet Mum
I was getting to like school, in fact it was fun
When I got older to a bigger school I had to move
For my maths, English and spelling I had to improve
One day I went there the teachers were making a fuss
Sit down Cousins and take your eleven plus
When I got the results through, I had failed the test
Thank God no grammar school even though I tried my best
Hailsham Secondary Modern was where I was sent
First day I got the slipper for my punishment
The next four years I spent all I could learning
Soon be time to leave and my keep to start earning
Now I have left I can remember Dad's advice
He was right, school days are the best of your life

R Cousins

My First Barman

My friend was eighteen
I was not
I was seventeen
And could have been shot

We walked into the bar
So big and bold
You should have heard
What we were told

'I'll just serve you'
The barman sung
'But not your friend,
He's much too young'

He looked at me
When he said that
I just ran
My friend just sat.

Charles Stewart

Bonfire Night

It is a cold clear starry night
The bonfires are alight
Sausages sizzling in the pan
Burgers ready for eating
Onions are being cooked
Everyone is definitely hooked

Excitement begins to grow
Waiting for the fireworks to glow
Children with sparklers, holding them tight
Mother is watching making sure they are alright
Fountains sending sparks like snow
Catherine wheels spinning round

Rockets shooting into the sky
Great bouquets glittering bright
Red, gold, green and silver
On this firework night
Lighting the sky for all to see
This day started in history

Looking at the children with eyes so bright
Their smiling faces
A spectacular sight
On this bonfire night.

Irene Pierce

My First Granddaughter's Wedding

Come to my house -
Warming party she said
Everyone's welcome
She said
So I washed by face
Put on my best clothes
Wore my shoes that
Showed my toes
Hired a taxi and
Arrived in style
Everyone there
And after a while
Granddaughter got us
All together
But not to talk about
The weather
I've got something
To tell you
I hope you'll be glad
I got married this
Morning
And you've all be had
It's not a house warming
Party at all
It's a wedding reception
So all have a ball
And we did.

M Wise

Barbara's Gifts

But once to stand beneath life's sky and wondered not on reasons
why,
but once to wait upon the word of songs once sung,
of souls once heard.
But once to stand in twilight's dawn then greet it
not with sorrows drawn,
these are the gift in dreams to be that thou has brought to set me free.
To walk, to run, to seek the sky, where eagles roam and roses die,
to whisper then a single word, that neither dark or day hath heard.
To stare upon a distant star and reach it then like dreams that are.
These are the things her love hath brought, to starless nights, to a
soul that sought. But once did I then touch her soul and ferry it
where rainbows go, I placed it then upon the mount and taught it
things its tears could shout.
I treasured it as vision's rose and wrote its name in endless prose.
Last I gave its name to thee and with a sigh then set it free.
To answer then the many ifs thy self did bring to me as gifts.

Kim Davenport

Remembering

I remember the first day at school.
The crying and waving to mothers
When they left us at school gates.
The pushing and shoving to hang up our coats.
Learning all sorts of things
To help along life's highways.

I remember the first day at work,
The hustle and bustle of office life.
Travelling backwards and forwards,
People rushing everywhere,
And proud of the first pay packet.

I remember the first date, the first kiss,
The very first dance and evening dress.
I remember the wedding and honeymoon,
The first home, the first child.
The first baby teeth and steps.
Excitement and pleasure,
The memories to treasure.

Meriel J Brown

My First Love

It's not been long
Nearly a year I think
But me and you, we are made to be together,
It feels as though I've known you my whole lifetime.
You have made me truly happy.
You've given me so much love and care,
Supported me through all the bad times,
Things that have affected us both.
So whenever you need me,
You can count on me, cause I promise you
I'll always be there.
We have found each other,
And I know we will stick together,
As you truly are the one for me.
I love you
And I'm looking forward to the future we have together.

Alison Fewins

Don't Let Go, Dad!

Shaky wheels and wobbly legs
Tongue held fast between his teeth
His fists are clenched on gleaming chrome
The excitement mounting breath by breath

It's time to go

A solid hand holds the saddle steady
And a loving voice says 'Now -
Push with your feet on those pedals son.
I've got you, don't worry, it's fun'

He builds up speed and calls
'Don't let go'
'I'm here' comes back the cry
'Keep pedalling son, you're doing so well
This is wonderful for your first try'

Then suddenly he feels the wind whistle past
And the voice begins to fade
He's alone, he's free and he's riding his bike

'Oh, how good it is to be me!'

Janet Munnings

My First Love

I remember my first girlfriend,
She was blonde with eyes of blue.
She didn't wear any fancy clothes,
Nor any make-up too.

One day when we were walking,
I whispered in her ear,
'You know how much I love you,
Will you marry me next year?'

Then I put my arms around her,
And kissed her tenderly.
She said 'I didn't realise
How much you cared for me.'

She smiled and said 'I love you,
But I think that we should wait,
You see you're only ten years old,
And me, I'm only eight.'

Brian Saunders

Young Love/First Time

Rhona by name,
Oh! What a dame,
She could fight like a man
And didn't give a damn.

Her lips tasted like cherries,
When we kissed at the berries,

Our hearts were pledged for life,
and
When you're both five,

That's a long, long time.

William A B Mennie

My First And Only . . . Dog

My dog is black,
he is a cocker-spaniel,
he takes a nap
near the fire.

His name is Jock,
he is very curly,
he barks when there's a knock,
even if it's me.

If you lay on the floor,
he licks you all over,
he scratches at the door
when he wants to go out.

Dannika Webber (11)

Lusty Love

The very first time I saw you,
I could not believe my eyes,
That someone across the water,
Would ask me out that night.
I pondered with the message,
That was passed to me,
But afterwards I wondered,
Was it all right for me!
My feelings were aroused
At the thought of going out
I put my best frock on
And off to town I went.
And there you were - a-playing
In the gig that night.
How smart and warm your smile was
Across the dim light,
I thought! He's not bad looking,
Talented - and smart.
Conservative and cool in fact.
Curly hair to shoulder length,
All shining in the light.
How lucky I was to have
Taken the date that night.
The memories I treasure
And the love you showed to me
Will stay with me forever
Until you return to me.

M Griffiths

A Man's Best Friend
(Tribute to Kielley)

So many years we spent together
Those days of sun, and stormy weather
Happy days and times of sadness,
Through them all you brought me gladness.

You seldom gave me cause to frown
And picked me up if I felt down
Such loyalty you rarely find
With friendships of the human kind.

More than a pet was meant to be
You were one of the family
And every member loved your ways
You truly brightened up our days.

Time took its toll as years went by
My greying hair, your poorly eye
You left my world, aged seventeen
And went to find, new pastures green.

From pup to parting faithful friend
You shared my life up to the end
And some day when life's burdens free me
I'll meet you somewhere else 'Dear Kielley'.

Kevin D Clapson

A Mother's Promise

Such overwhelming love I felt the day that you were born
They placed you in my arms
I cried, those tears were tears of joy
Those tiny fingers wrapped around the hand that held you dear
And as you slept
I shared your dreams
And whispered in your ear . . .
'I promise I will love you, and help in every way
I'll be your friend
I'll care for you
I'm your mother I'm here to stay
My thoughts of you
And prayers for you I'll carry for all time
You're my daughter and I'll always treasure
The day God made you mine.'

Tracey Klenk

A Fresh New Day

First thing you wake to a fresh new day,
Very happy to see the first sun's ray.
Glad to face a bright new morn,
Sun is rising to kiss the dawn.
We all have problems, sometimes it's a struggle,
And life seems to be in one big muddle.

When we are kids we live in a dream,
Nothing as perfect as it always seems.
When we grow up and problems appear,
Very often reduces us to sadness and tears.

Then we have spells and things seem so right,
Wish they could last, forever be all right.
We'd all like to sail along through life,
With as little problems, that cause trouble and strife.

So when I wake up to a fresh new day,
I give thanks to my Maker as I kneel and pray.
I'm alive and kicking, and a new poem's on the way,
I'm so grateful and happy to live for each day.

Linda Garner

First Sap Rising

The fearless age of nine compelled me to climb
High into a mighty leafy tree,
Near to where Tarzan's trail used to be,
I deftly tied a hemp rope around a stout bough,
And prepared to hurl myself into the mid-summer sky,
Invincible courage wavered and I cast instead old
Dick Tracey's inquiring eye upon a mysterious man and woman,
Who, in moody gaze, were settling themselves comfortably
Into a flowing field of ripening wheat,
I really couldn't help but sit and stare, intrigued and bemused,
By all the rolling and moaning soon taking place down there,
The coupling pair spent frenzied time completing what
                                        comes naturally,
Then! Off they went with feelings vent never to be seen again,
I wandered, less innocent than before, to the flattened patch
                                        of choking wheat,
Joy upon joy fortune had followed me there,
Threepenny bits, shillings, florins, half-crowns and tanners
Galore, were lying at my jumping feet,
I fast became a millionaire gathering in my bountiful harvest bare,
'Off to the shops!' an instant thought, where I eagerly bought,
Pounds of sticky sweets and liquorice black,
I ambled home with smudged red face, pockets bulging and jaws
Straining to maintain the pace,
'What have you done? . . . Where have all these sweets come from?'
A disciplinarian father demanded angrily of me,
I couldn't bring myself to tell the truth about my explosive time of
milt and money,
Tears flowed like lashing rain but he boxed my ears just the same,
Being grounded had no effect,
Something strange but good had stirred within and remains still,
Along with the grey and ageing tree,
Which I still see through twinkled eye and always will.

Robert Henry Lonsdale

30th March In The Year 1941

I took my first job at the age of twelve
Selling copies of the Philadelphia Daily News Inquirer
That employment I held for only four days
Until I delivered papers for the Montgomery County Record
When I was at the age of eleven years old
Moved out of North Hills and into Abington Township
Between July and September of nineteen-eighty-eight
Mom and I headed up to Roslyn just the two of us
My first Warrington apartment was at twenty-two eighty-eight B
Walked downstairs to twenty-two eighty-eight A
Left the road/drive in nineteen-ninety-four
Just to return five years and one month later
November eighty-seven after turkey dinner
Made my international debut in Niagara Falls, Ontario, Canada
My visit lasted for sixty minutes
Would go back on the territory of Puerto Rico
Was my mother's first born child from my mother's first marriage
husband
My brother BJ was the second coming
His first trip outside of the USA
Was to The Projects of Cuban East LA
March ninety-eight employee of the month
Was award number one before award number two
On the twenty-eight of February in the year nineteen-ninety-nine
Got employee of the year right on time
This novel was about a first time for everything
Like in nineteen-ninety-three when I started to sing
I don't rap anymore because my skin is turning pale

Harry Swanger

For John Glenn
(This reflects on another first and is one of my hopes . . .)

Ol' John returned,
Coasting down the air currents
In his new fangled space glider:

'But I thought he drops down
In a capsule with a parachute . . .'
Mom said.

'No, no that was long ago . . .
It's better now.

Next time, you see 'em
Glide down - all the way from Mars
With their red rocks and Martian biomes -

Maybe it'll be our son . . .
Maybe this Ol' John will go with him . . .'
Dad said.

John A Mills

'Battle Of Britain' Baby

You should have seen mine;
Bombs dropping,
Dogs barking,
Babies yelling,
Mum sweating,
Midwife encouraging,
Baby arrives, howling.
Smiles and - yes! Fears.

Mum sits up and writes her cards . . .
. . . For her family and friends:-
'Sex: Weight and Date'
Seven stone eight,
What a whopper!
What a mistake!
A bundle of love . . .
. . . At seven *pounds* eight.

A Betty Harrison

Love Me

Monday cannot come too soon,
The chance of seeing you makes me swoon.

When I turn and see you there,
My world is lifted beyond compare.

Your beauty and your smiling way,
Lasts me throughout the day.

Love is such an easy game to play,
But mine for you will last forever and a day.

Thank you for the happiness you bring,
Yes this is truly spring.

Harry Chandra

First Glimpses
(Thoughts on After-Life)

What will it be like
in that other realm unknown,
when death has closed my eyelids
and the breath of life has flown?
Will there be shining light
beckoning from the dark beyond,
will there be a garden, flowers, trees,
bird-song, voices familiar or strange?

Will He be there to welcome me,
the One I have trusted so long;
or will He just look at me
as He once looked at St Peter,
knowing my innermost thoughts,
so that I dare not look!
Will there be love and forgiveness
and a sense of coming home?

Will they be there,
the friends I have known and loved,
my father and mother
who gave me birth;
the people I once cared for,
and those I have failed.
Will they be there to greet me
in loving friendship, joyfully renewed.

I have greatly loved
morning skies, blue and rain-washed,
sunsets with the burning colours of the dying sun,
mountains, green fields and rivers,
primrose-filled woods with violets growing on shady banks.
All those places where we walked and talked
amidst the kindly company of four-footed friends
prancing and dancing over the turf.

Will it be better even than these?

Beryl Johnson

Can One Love The Unlovable?

Can I love the unlovable? Can I hate the loveable?
Can I touch the untouchable? Can one love the unlovable?
I'm an endless questioner, and so you are! Can my love be hateful?
Can't the hateable be loveable? Can one love the unlovable?
Why do I claim to love Jean? What is loveable in her?
Is she intrinsically loveable? Can one love the unlovable?
Why do I claim to hate Josephine? What is unlovable in her?
Is she intrinsically unlovable? Can one love the unlovable?
Why do I claim to have different feelings for people? Why do I seem
happy when I see John?
Why do I seem sad when I see Joseph? Can one love the unlovable?
What makes some people loveable and some unlovable? Is the
loveability in the observer or in the observed?
Where is the source of the loveableness? Can one love the
unlovable?
One day, He said 'Love your enemies!' One man from Assisi kissed the
feet of a leper!
A woman in Calcutta befriended the dying homeless! Shouldn't one
love the unlovable?
Gandhi's satyagraha-the force of love, gave birth to non-violence.
He lived with the untouchables as children of God.
Jean Vanier an aristocratic philosopher made an alliance with
mental handicaps. Shouldn't one love the unlovable?
How do I feel when I'm considered loveable? How do I feel when I'm
considered unlovable?
How can I be loveable and unlovable at the same time? Shouldn't one
love the unlovable?
What makes me, me? Is it what I know of myself?
Is it what others know of me? Shouldn't one love the unlovable?

Human love is logical, an apparent love. We love what appears to be loveable!

Divine love is ontological, we are loved because we are. Shouldn't one love the unlovable?

When one encounters the being who is love par excellence, the loveable-unlovable distinction withers.

Can one love the unlovable? Shouldn't one love the unlovable?

Wilbert Gobbo

A Step In Time

The day is warm
and sleeveless,
we walk as strangers against
the tide of strangers.

The sun brings
laughter to its shadows.

In time, we are in step,
our wordless march
draws us together,
the touch of arm
upon arm makes
the event inevitable.

My arm around your shoulders
means no harm.

Our ways part,
the sorrow shows,
our smiles depart.

My hand outstretched -
as yours withdraws.

Michael A Fenton

The First Cry

From the first moment you sense you are 'enceinte' you are waiting,
Whether you are pleased or distressed about the one you are creating.
Life has you in its hands controlling every step you make
Doubling up the perils of life you both have at stake.
Your fears or doubts may be lessened by the joy of anticipation
Which can be eased to some extent by a happy expectation.
Subtle changes occur in your form and your mental processes
And your emotions may need more sensitive caresses.
There are landmarks to pass which present short term hurdles;
The three month danger-point, the first kick and disposal
of your girdles.
Your progress is measured in months and an eye on the forecasted
date
Until at last you are close and wondering whether the babe will be
late.
A few more anxious days with eyes that are rarely completely dry
Until at last the final effort rewarded by that *First Heart-warming cry!*

Allen Jessop

My Definition Of Love

Love is tender, love is kind,
The eyes of love, can be open or blind.
Love is caring, love is sharing,
Love is precious, never comparing.
Love's in you and I,
Love can make you happy or cry.
Love is honest, love is true,
I hope the love lasts for me and you.
Love is patient, I'm here waiting,
I'm here forever anticipating.
Love is of give and take,
If we get together, I pray our hearts
We'll never break.
Love's not self-righteous,
If we get closer, of you I'll always make a fuss.
The love I feel for you deep inside,
Is hard to comprehend,
To your every need, I'll lovingly tend.

Karen Stephens

No Longer A Dream

Did you long for a place to go,
Somewhere out of reach, that no one knows,
Was it in the mind, when you were young,
Always there beside you when you were in the sun.

As you grew up, did you say,
Mainly to yourself, there might be a way,
Was it in your mind, as years went by,
Or did you just forget, in the passing time,

Later in life, you knew it was there,
Dreams and aspirations mean that you care,
Always live in hope and you will find,
Dreams become reality, sometimes.

But you made it, hear what I say,
Standing in the shadows, on a special day,
You made it and now you have seen,
That, what you always wanted, is no longer a dream.

John Cook

My First Day At Boarding School

The journey from Newcastle was a nightmare, I was eight.
Three hundred miles to London, and the train was running late.
I bid a brave farewell to Mum on King's Cross railway station
Then off I went with Matron to an alien destination.

It was in the early evening when we reached Bexhill-on-Sea
A pretty, southern seaside town would now be home to me.
The Avenue seemed endless as I dragged my weary feet
To a large Victorian building, in the unaccustomed heat.

The door was huge and heavy, like the portal of a church.
As I opened it and peeped inside, I felt my stomach lurch.
The entrance was foreboding, it unleashed a thousand fears.
I was choking back emotion, but would not give way to tears.

Matron stood beside me in that gloomy entrance hall
As I gazed around in horror with my back against the wall.
My hands were washed, my case unpacked, and then with undue
haste
Escorted to the dining room, for food was not to waste.

I cannot eat spaghetti; it's a dish I really hate
And I watched with trepidation as it writhed upon my plate.
The day had been traumatic; this was just the final blow
But my troubles really started when I cried out 'No, No, No!'

They didn't seem to understand the torment I was in,
As they tried to make me eat it, what a sinner, what a sin!
Food was meant to be consumed in 1952,
But I was eight, and in distress, my turmoil grew and grew.

Resistance with the pasta brought me punishment, and bed.
I cried myself to sleep that night, with blankets overhead.
The silent tears of inward grief were not for Matron's ears
The battle lines were drawn that night; I would not show my fears.

Doreen Hanley

My First Love And My First Dream

You were the first person I ever adored
The one that I thought I would love evermore
The one that I held in the highest esteem
You were my first love and you were my first dream

You were the first one that took notice of me
Together forever I thought we would be
You were my first sunshine and my first moonbeam
You were my first love and you were my first dream

And you were the first to make my heart skip a beat
And you were the first one I saw as elite
You were the one perfect and you were the cream
You were my first love and you were my first dream

But then somewhere else you decided to stray
And with you, you took my excitement away
My heart broke in two and my face lost its beam
Now you're my first broken love and my first broken dream

David John Dunbar

To My First Grandson

Hi there, little man, and welcome!
Grandson, son and brother all in one.
My heart is full as
I embrace you with my fondest love
And give my thanks to God on high,
While you, unknowing and sublime,
Lie easy in your mother's arms.
But be assured of this, my dear wee pal,
That you and Freya - oh so dear -
Mean everything to me as I gaze down
Upon your small, yet manly, frame.
And as you grow that frame to fill
So, too, your love will grow as great as mine.
'Tis not the moment now to think of what may be,
But sure I am of this, my bonny lad -
From now, you are the *bearer of the name!*

Angus W MacDonald

My Firstborn

My first baby's birth, was full of emotion,
Trepidation, panic fright and commotion,
Waking in labour, into my sister's bedroom I crept,
Two pairs of feet, which are hers, I thought as I wept,
I arrived at the hospital, was put in a ward,
Writhing and yelling, the bed was rock hard,
Like nothing on earth was the pain I was in,
In came a nurse, whatever's the din,
Down to the labour ward, no one in sight,
I must have looked an awful fright,
My long hair done in pincurls, some hadn't stayed in,
In came a lady, on her face a grin,
Would you like some tea dear, I gave her a glare,
How can I drink tea in this state, you stupid mare
Get out of my sight, I heard myself yell,
I felt a great whoosh, from somewhere below, panicking I rang the
bell,
In rushed the midwife, I cried my baby's been born,
It's alright she said, your waters have gone,
I had a beautiful girl, just before sunrise,
I awoke sometime later to my sweet baby's cries,
I combed my hair, in came the lady at whom I had yelled,
I said I'm sorry I shouted, as my hand she held,
You look so much better, bet you'd like that tea now,
My world was at peace, after the pain and the row,
My firstborn is now forty years,
The years have passed by, with laughter and tears,
After four more children, her birth wasn't the worst,
From all of my memories, I remember hers first,
My children and grandchildren, are the joys of my life,
Joy and happiness, far outweighing the strife.

Patricia Barrett

First Day

Between the life and death of man, there is a time
When pain is forgotten, all joy is unknown.
Shadows dance, yet no light shone.
Light is there and yet no darkness.
Death is there and yet no fear.
Welcome sleep and yet awakening
Gently slide yet hasten on.
Death is calling. Life, an echo
Fades away and now is gone.

Farewell, farewell to death and sorrow
Slow decay that binds the soul.
Parting now will break the bondage
Loss of half and yet, now whole.

Gillian Hare-Scott

For Bessie

She stayed beside me more than fifty years,
The first love of my life: she was so young
And beautiful, a shining star among
The throng in which she moved. Her lively peers,
All schoolgirls then, to me could not compare.
Ambitious, bright and free, she would have none
Of lads like me. I lost her: she was gone,
I knew not where. Then came the hideous glare
Of war to transform lives. A quirk of fate,
Bizarre encounter, brought her to my side,
Where she remained, my lovely faithful bride,
Through all alarms; until at last the weight
Of Parkinson's dread plague gave her release
From suffering to let her sleep in peace.

Frank Littlewood

If
(To Joyce)

If I could kindle a flame in your heart
To bring purpose to my life
Never more for it's to part
Could you be my wife
If I did honour and protect you my love
With tender loving care - undefined
If I could do all those things above
Could you bear my child
If I could with all sincerity provide
Companionship for you my dear
And explain this feeling deep inside
Could you be my wife

Billy Rose

My First And Only Love

The rain came down with such determination,
A sweeping gust of wind took umbrellas in the air,
To say I was wet was an understatement
It all looked like a comic sketch.
Then my eye caught a movement,
A head bent low looking through the window
A most beautiful smile and eyes that spoke.
I tried to walk past but was all in a fluster
I got myself caught on rose bush thorns,
The face from the window was then stood beside me
The wind and the rain didn't matter at all.

He took my arm gently and warmly requested
That tea for two would be nice
I felt like a schoolgirl, and just mumbled, thank you,
That was the start of my life.
This first love was as sweet as the nectar
That came from beautiful flowers,
His voice was the soft gentle breeze of the air.
Although I had lived a fulfilling life
Before this love I met,
This was my first my only love,
And this was to last the rest of my life.
We weren't teenagers or young starry-eyed,
We weren't what you call middle aged,
But love is love no matter what age,
Even the first time around.

Mary Neill

Untitled

The beach strewn
with leathered weed,
the sieve of sea and sand
lasting, passing in their need
for nature's perfected
movements. Stones cragged
by the North Sea's cutting winds
carving into ragged
relics nature's memories
hidden in its petrine
mysteries, treasured by
boyish hands tracking
every history line.
Every wave is in praise
of those who in awe hold
such mysteries beyond
their hands and are bold
enough to listen to the
roaring, whispering waves
and through each shell reach
into its silent, sounding caves.

Jack Clancy

My First!

My first was unforgettable
Though happening in ages past
A memory of awesome achievement
A savoured moment meant to last

The years have come and gone
In fleeting, dwindling time
My first is always with me
Unlike the clock's ticks, with bygone chime

My first was meant to stay with me
Hazed memories cloud my mind
Was my achievement all that great?
Did it somehow benefit, mankind?

White hair that's left, adorns me
Wrinkles scar my furrowed brow
Grey cells that were once efficient
Are less in number now

Recollection now eludes me
My first, I can't recall
Was *my first* achievement with
My wife, or someone different *after all?*

Francis L A Farmer

My First

I used to pass her house each day
when in my early teens:
I slowed my pace, I gazed within
but didn't have the means
to ask her for a date with me.
I heard her play L'amour',
the sound of love caressed my heart,
and pangs of love full sure.
Then one Sunday morning late,
her organ duties done,
when homeward bound she spoke to me -
our tale of two begun!
Soon dances in the local hut
would feelings great bestir:
her parents took her home each time
should anything occur.
Alas, the war took me away
and letters had to do
to tell her how I missed her so
and be forever true.
Then back again to Blighty's shore
and soon we tied the knot;
three loving families appeared -
a caring, loving lot.
It's more than sixty years ago
that Gran first spoke to me.
She'll be my *first* and only love
for all eternity.

Owen Edwards

My First

Rhyming comes quite naturally,
God's gift to me was free;
Though not blessed with punctuation skill,
I admit this worried me.
So after lots of dithering,
A finally arrived -
At a creative writing class,
To conquer lack of skills I strived.
My tutor is an author,
Rhymes she doesn't write;
Assignments were mainly just for prose,
Though producing poetry was alright.
I struggled many months with prose,
Often falling back on rhyme;
With lots of encouragement all round,
Surely there must come a time?
Long after I had left the class.
Assignments I rewrote;
Until the day I felt elation,
I've got it, yes! I thought.
Punctuation no longer worries me,
With it I don't feel cursed;
My short story was accepted,
A published triumph this; my first!

Ivy Squires

I Let Him In

I had a first time in my life
It was the day I found Jesus Christ
He made my heart swing with all love
He turned my all around
Yes my first love now is Jesus
For in him new life I've found
My burdens he lifts from my soul
He is here for me when I am weak
I was so pleased when I found Jesus
Tears flowed with the joys I reap
Now he is my first in all things
How ever could I let him go
For Jesus took away all of my sins
For this I just love him so
I never lived until that day
That day when Jesus came into my heart
And washed all my nasty sins away
I do not live for self - not anymore
I live for Jesus - who opened my heart's door
Each morning like the sun I rise
Looking up to his bright blue skies
And at night I talk away
As knowing him so close I love to pray
Yes I had a first time and it's going to last
He is the one now who shares my all
I'm so pleased I let him in through my heart's door

Marion Staddon

My First Love

We met, full of delight,
when we were living in a vacuum.
We climbed Castle Hill, sharing
emotions hidden from reality.
Every year we promised to return
together to the highest battlement
to ask if we remained unchained,
if doubt and fears had crept
upon us in the months between.

Thoughts fill my heart and seek to blend
the past and future into memory.
On that castle on a hill you and I
were alone yet one beneath the sun.
Fields slope from hedges and lanes,
secretly behind green trees.
So wide are limits of this place
it is a refuge to renew our vows
and makes us glad to be alive.

Climbing winding stairs shadows rest
uninvited, withered for centuries.
Now I know a ring accepted will seal our vows.
Gazing on open landscape
trees stand out like toys beneath.
Both our hearts are stilled
by glorious landscape and peace unfolding
to far distances.
Your hand is firm forever on my arm.

N Reeves

New York, New York
(First impressions)

Civilisation, on a roll

Tamed land, testing its soul on
Wall Street. Nine-to-fivers in a rush
to beat fellow survivors to the internet,
earn the right to take a shower,
put up their feet, do the town
(on credit). On the sidewalk,
a steel band, marketing
the Promised Land

Civilisation, on a roll

Central Park, good for a stroll
when the heat's on; oases of quiet water
like cameos of family life sparkling
in the sun. St Thomas's but a stone's
throw away on the Avenue open
all hours - a Gothic charm among
Fortune's towers, to office hours
no thrall

Civilisation, on a roll

R N Taber

My First Dog

A faithful friend I found
in you always there to greet
my presence from wherever
I had been.
To the fields we sometimes
roamed by the stream
down by the valley
in the stream you used
to swim.
I remember getting
wet when you shook
the water off.

A Labrador with skin
jet black, loves to lie
by my fire when the winter
turns so cold
he knows it's best
by far to stay indoors
until the morning
light turns bright

Ernie Cummings

First Love

Your smiling face,
Your gentle ways
Made me love
You more each day
You were my first love
A love so true
I know I'll never forget you
Looking in the mirror
Checking make-up okay
Waiting for you darling
I've been keyed up all day
And then at last you're here
My heart is pitter pattering away
As you tell me you love me
And that you will
Forever stay.

Davina Glaser

New Harvest

Inside me, there is a welling up of energy,
but I do not know where to send it.
The light hits me from another galaxy,
colliding, asking new questions.
These switching lights and flashing emotions,
distance and myopic supposition.
I would like to reply, right now.
I wish to balance the speeding light,
with an inner coalescence.
There is a message in this engagement,
but what language are we all using?
This never ending stimulation.
All I want to do is say thank you.
Transmit my sincerity, let it grow,
free to mingle with other seeds.
Harvesting new truth, for the first time.

J Walker

Love Heart Sweeties In The Classroom

I was eight
She was eight and a quarter
An older woman
I opened the packet
And gave her 'Be Mine'
She blushed
And gave me 'Sugar You'
My heart skipped a beat
And my stomach felt funny
I gave her 'Sweetheart'
More blushing
Too much for eight year olds
She opened the packet further
And gave me 'I Love You'
I sighed, stammered and choked
'Me And You' I gave her in return
Young love is great, but
First love is sweeter than sherbet sweets.

Ian Speirs

The Year Of The Scourge

Red blanket on the window,
Disinfectant by the door.
A sign for all to keep away,
According to the law.

The siren of the ambulance,
Screeching down the street.
A child is carried from the house,
Covered in a sheet.

Oh no! Oh no! The neighbours shout,
That dreaded plague is here,
Scarlet Fever's back again,
For yet another year.

The year was 1938,
A time I'll not forget,
I was that child they carried out,
Caught in that viral net.

Isolated in a ward,
My bed behind a screen.
Visitors were not allowed,
For infection was extreme.

Marshall Collins

To Count The Feathers On Its Wings
(Poem based on memories of the first 24 hours
after the author had a cataract operation)

It seemed strange, waiting for the first sign of light,
like removing a thin film and suddenly once faded images
have round and sharp contours.

Then the searing of white
especially window frames and ledges
seeming to sharpen
where a line began and another one ended.

Best was the novelty
of counting, from a distance, branches on a tree.
Then, down at the harbour,
getting so close to a gull to count the feathers on its wings.

Jules A Riley

Late, But Not Too Late

First love, no, but last love, yes!
At eighty years I find it fair,
It is as love has ever been
A wonder of an endless sheen.
After the years I should know,
For I have been well blest,
But this last dream is very fair
A girl who once I knew is there,
Not girl, but woman, sweetly she has grown
And we who once were old, are young:
The world is fair, the flowers are blooming,
Sunshine everywhere, thank God for this.
This wonder he has brought.

Fred Curd

First Flight

Excitement at fever pitch
Will it go without a hitch?
Taxi late - where has it gone?
I'll miss my plane - I feel forlorn.

At last it comes, I'm on my way.
Arrive at the airport and join the fray.
Such a queue at the check-in desk
I'm so on edge - it's my turn next.

A cup of tea is what I need.
I drink it up with frantic speed.
To departure lounge I make my way.
I'm lost again - I've gone astray.

My boarding pass I cannot find
Oh! Help, I might be left behind.
Yes, here it is I'm safe to go.
I wait and wait, it's all so slow.

At last they let us on the plane.
A window seat, I can't complain.
The engines rev, what a noise they make.
We're off the ground, for goodness sake!

The nice young girl gave me a sweet
And then a drink and food to eat.
It's such a rush to eat in time
The packs to open - I'm far behind.

Then fasten seat belts, we're coming in
The engines making such a din.
I thank the staff when going out
A lovely trip, without a doubt.

I follow on where others go
I'm getting there, I'm not so slow.
The cases all coming swinging round
It takes a while but *my* case I've found.

To the exit I must go
My daughter will be there I know.
Delighted thoughts I shall not lack
For soon I shall be flying back.

Dorothy Hill Bradshaw

My First Perm

Would you like to hear a story
Of the day I had my first perm?
It happened back in the thirties,
And it really made me squirm.

I was a young girl of sixteen,
With hair that was oh! so straight,
And tho I really longed for curls,
My mum said 'You'll have to wait.'

One day she gave into my pleas
And booked an appointment for me,
I didn't know what to expect,
But know I felt full of glee.

Inside the shop I looked in awe,
At the implements that were there,
Were they going to use them on me,
To get rid of my straight hair?

The scissors snipped, my hair fell off,
I felt drowned with all the water,
On went the papers and curlers,
Too late for 'Did I oughta'.

Ammonia then was plastered on
Then the instrument of torture,
When I was strung up high as high,
I bet it thought, 'I've gotcha'.

After about four hours had gone,
Curlers off, hair well washed and passed,
Styled and set and then told - 'Now look'
I felt beautiful - at last.

Isobel Crumley

184

First And Last Love

Midst these dim gardens where my
Heart 'doth' glean its rest
Where memories of past days return
Where my feet tread oh so softly lest
In among the primrose and the fern
They wake again the torments of past love
A love long gone, a love ne'er to return
This is where my heart can live again
Away from all the cares and jeers of man
Where sweeter thoughts may ease my heart's harsh pain
Thoughts that end where all my tears began
This is where in half-remembered youth
The seeds of springtime love were deeply sown
Where shining eyes blazed with the light of truth
And banished every care that I had known
Oh 'fool' that thought you ever could forget
When memory is etched in every stone.

A Kerman

The First Wage

My very first pay cheque,
Oh wow! What a thrill;
A minuscule film part,
I remember it still.
The first step to stardom,
My name up in lights,
I set off for Pinewood
To conquer the heights:
But wardrobe and make-up
Quite soon put me wise,
A surgical mask covered all
But my eyes.
The part I was playing?
A hospital nurse
Assisting a surgeon:
Things couldn't be worse:
I thought I had ten lines
But soon I had none:
Another girl pinched them
How smartly 'twas done!
She and the male lead
Were having a fling,
Naive little me
Didn't notice a thing.
So, my debut - disaster!
Many lessons I learned.
But that wage cheque was special,
The first one I'd earned.

Corinne Lovell

First Love

We married when she was only twenty
And looked to life to give us plenty
I've loved her now for forty years
Through happiness, laughter sometimes sadness and tears
Throughout all times she's always been there
Looking after me through each passing year
She gave to me four children
That made me see
That there's more to life
Than the quest for money
We've had our good times, we've had our bad
We've had years of happiness, a few that's been sad
I took a girl and made her my wife
She's shown to me the joys of life
I love her more with each passing day
Words can't express what she means to me
Lover, friend, mother, great company
She's been all these things and many more
That young girl, my wife, who I adore
If I had millions, they could never bring
The happiness she brought with a wedding ring
My wife what more can I say
I'll love you till my dying day

Ernest Myers

First Visit To New York

A million feet - a multitude of faces
A human stew of different races
At Times Square, an enormous queue
Half price show tickets there for you
To be purchased only on the day
For all theatres on or off Broadway
A group of youngsters from different lands
Are singing hymns happily holding hands
Rockerfeller Centre folk sipping drink
As they watch the skaters on the rink.
You want coffee - flavoured or de-caff
Is it black, creamer- or half and half?
Eggs over-easy, hash or home fries?
Add maple syrup - there's no surprise
Tit-bits to tempt every kind of taste
In the land of plenty - and of waste!
Horsedrawn carriages trot to and fro
How the taxis miss them I don't know
In Central Park trees are a delight
With the playground and zoo in sight
The very top of 'World Trade' beckons
Hundred and six floors in thirty seconds
The standing in line was worth the wait
When gazing down at the 'Empire State'
At night hear helicopters overhead
Viewing the city when you're in bed
See the green 'Statue of Liberty'
Impressively rising from the sea
It bids you return some other day
To the teeming heart of the USA

Valerie Goble

First Love

Green leaves falling, silent as a whisper
thoughts drifting back to my youth,
autumn of year, autumn of life
a gentle kiss on a loving mouth
remembering sweet days aglow
and long dark nights, so slow
dark eyes staring, passion sharing
dreams to come, hopes so bold
now lay shattered, hearts gone cold.

Cheryl Mann

Your Eyes, Your Smile, Your Touch

Your eyes are saying things no spoken words could say
They talk to me of love, that's come to stay
There, I see fields of sparkling amber grain
Kissed by the soft, sweet, gentle summer rain

Your smile, it tells me all I want to know
It says you want me, it says you love me so
Your heart's an open book there for all to see
Joy and sorrow, you can't hide, when you look at me

Your touch it says so many things to me
Your warm embrace, helps to set my spirit free
When your heart's beating ever close to mine
I'm in paradise, I'm in heaven for a time.

Your eyes, your smile, your touch
I love them oh so much!

Karl Jakobsen

The Timepiece

When weary I climb into bed.
My aching joints refuse to sleep.
In my head chapters of my life lie deep.
I turn back pages to Christmases past.
In a cardboard box among my dolls at last.
My first ever wrist-watch, I thought silver and black.
Chromium plated it swamped my tiny wrist.
I gazed in awe and felt such bliss.
My enchantment with the expanding strap.
I knew it couldn't really last.
I wound it up both night and day.
Until the winder came away.
And then the magical ticking stopped.
I hardly ever took it off, the glass was cracked.
And still I kept it long after that.
In a small cardboard box my first wrist-watch.

Ethel Oates

Tydraw

I will never forget the first time I stumbled on Tydraw
It was the prettiest house that I ever saw
Nestling down a lane what a splendid scene
Covered in bushes trees and grass so green

The people who owned it did not seem to care
It really was run down and in need of repair
I knew I had to buy it from day one
Looking after it would be a pleasure and so much fun

It had high ceilings and dark oak beams
It really was the answer to all my dreams
All over the house it had wooden floors
Also it had a long and narrow corridor

The garden was run down and a terrible sight
But in my mind I could see flowers colourful and bright
Tulips pussy willlows and bumble bees
Birds singing on the branches of the blossom trees

I can still remember the first time I ever saw Tydraw
Now it really is the prettiest house I ever saw
It is not run down and in need of repair
The people who live in it really care

D A Fieldhouse

A Book At Bedtime

I go to bed and I take a book,
Sometimes it's a book on what to cook.
The other night the book that I got
Was all about love of which I've had a lot.
I read these books and I feel so glad,
It could have been my story and all the love I have had.
Wouldn't it be sad if you had missed all this
And didn't know the bliss of your first kiss,
The tingle in your feet as you go on your date,
Not wanting to be early, not wanting to be late
And turning the corner and seeing him there,
Trying to be cool and pretending you don't care.
Then he looks at you and you look at him
And your own love story is about to begin.
Next thing you know the book is on the floor
And when you wake up your love is there no more.

Ennis Nosko-Smith

The New Baby

The new baby pink and soft lay at its mother's breast
The long hours of labour, all she wants is rest
Those little hands so perfect, blue eyes and toothless grin
Oh! He is so beautiful, father's nose and mother's chin
She gazes at him lovingly so fragile in her arms
Longing to protect him from all of life's harms
Trying to imagine what his future might hold
Whether he will be handsome, big and bold
Or slim and delicate always catching cold
Maybe he will be clever and climb the ladder high
Perhaps he will fail exams no matter how he try
As she lays him in the cot all blue and neat
She tickles tenderly the tiny little feet
Tucking him in safely she mouths a silent prayer
Offering her beloved child into God's loving care

Veronica Quainton

Water Fool

The first time I went camping, not a day it didn't rain,
The sun was off on holiday too, that was very plain.

There seemed to be a surfeit, of the dreaded H_2O,
It always seemed to come, alas it never seemed to go.

It's called inclement weather, (and other things beside),
And soon I felt like King Canute, trying to stem the tide.

It hadn't been so wet since Noah built his ark,
I think I would have felt at home, if I had been a shark.

I didn't go home a healthy brown, instead I was quite blue,
Why wet weather follows me, I haven't got a clue.

When I got home my friends would ask, 'Was the weather fine?'
And I just had to tell them, the sun refused to shine.

Then some would call me, 'Water Lou', and ask me 'Where's
your gamp?'
And said 'I hear your holiday was just a trifle damp.'

And then would you believe it, the sun came out once more,
It was just one more example of the well known 'Murphy's Law'.

Joe Pester

The Mini (Our First Car)

Our 1962 Mini was more textured matte than gloss
The sliding windows didn't, due to cultivated moss
The glove box held salt and vinegar so there could be no doubt
That we would lack for nothing when we decided to eat 'out'.

The engine gleamed, it looked brand new, it didn't get much wear
Ten miles in any direction, as much as we would dare
The manual said 'use 4 star' but we ran that car for free
So rarely was it running, its main power source was me!

I pushed that car mile after mile, a marriage of skin and chrome
Sometimes struggling into life, at others towed sadly home
A toolbox? Pointless luggage! Prayers - our only hope,
Good walking shoes, coins for the phone and a length of strong,
thick rope.

Every weekend, come rain or shine, we'd fill her up with oil
Top up the radiator, for it was sure to boil
Third party cover only, to ensure the minimum cost
One lone windscreen wiper, the other - tragically lost.

One summer's day, to our despair, she gave her final kick
Dancing days gone, couldn't do a *slow, slow* and no hope of a *quick.*
The doctor's diagnosis - terminal engine fever
'Look around, you won't do better than that nice little '67 Viva . . .'

Sally Jobson

First

Oh gosh, oh golly
Oh heavens above
Oh me, oh my
Oh my sweet love

Oh goodness me
Oh great despair
I've just found
My first grey hair!

. . . is that a wrinkle?

Sarah Bell

That First Touch Of Magic

I remember the time - 'twas a fine Mother's Day
When my daughter and husband had something to say
'You're invited to tea' - a pressing request
Just two happy families, with no outside guest.

The table looked grand with lashings of food
A nice glass of wine put us all in the mood
It was some celebration that we all had to share
Excitement was rife, it buzzed in the air.

'We have something to tell you' my daughter began
'Would you be happy if you were a gran?'
Happy! I tell you, I whooped in the air
Got enthusiastic and fell off my chair!

Well, the months passed us by and my daughter got bigger
Waving goodbye to her curvaceous figure
As happy a couple as ever you'd see
And glowing with health - this mother-to-be.

Then the big day arrived, and our grandchild was born
A dear little girl with the first light of dawn
Her mother was resting, was having a 'spell'
And they told us that father was 'doing quite well'

A child filled with secrets, eyes of wisdom had she
I am sure she smiled very special for me
But this lass gave no favours 'twixt one and the other
For she smiled just the same at her other grandmother.

Three granddaughters on, and I love them all dearly
Each 'special birth' I remember so clearly
Experience has taught us, we are now fully versed
But - with a small touch of magic - I remember the first.

Barbara Davies

Your First Steps

Your first steps were a miracle,
You tottered towards me,
Faltering, stumbling.

I held my breath in wonder
As you came closer,
My arms were open
Ready to welcome you

And then you were there
Triumphant confidant
And the memory was
Imprinted on my heart
Forever.

Dianne Core

My First

Long ago in '21
When I was nine years minus one
I 'trod the boards' of theatre old
(It's now a shop where buns are sold)
'Mayday-in-Welladay' 'twas named
An operette for children claimed.
Each year, our school to celebrate
Pancake Tuesday's variable date
Presented us in song and dance
And, incidentally did enhance
My thespian dream of acting fame
(Aspiring not be a 'dame')
But to delight those who had paid
And thus to merit accolade
From parents, teachers and my peers
From 'Theatre Royal's Gallery-Tiers'.
Recalling, now I'm pleased to tell
I was cast as - a bluebell -
A fairy dressed in azure blue
With song to sing and dance to do.
Stage-fright afflicted vocal tone
As words-of-song away had flown.
But teacher's prompt restored my nerve
I made my exit to deserve
Both reprimand plus 'toffee award'
For fairy bluebell's 'treading-the-board'.

Frances Cox

Bedfellows

I knew you, friend, from early days,
    And loved you from the start.
Companion of my childhood's ways,
    We seldom were apart.
When winter nights were cold and dim
    My childhood's bed I'd share,
And if I woke from frightening dream,
    Thankful, I'd find you there.
As days went by and I grew up
    An interval there came.
My teenage self no longer sought
    Its loyalty to proclaim.
But as the years went streaming by
    Too fast for keeping track
Came early friendship wistfully,
    Scarce noticed, stealing back.
Though decades since we parted and
    Still dearer friends came there
To share my life, beloved cats -
    First love, my teddy bear!

Kathleen M Hatton

Untitled

My 1st love I married
My 1st death I cried
All my children come 1st
In all of these I've tried

A 1st I won for baking
A 1st I won for jam
Most of all, I now stand tall
With a 1st of what I am.

My major great achievement
A poem, the 1st I wrote
I sent it to be published
Then waited with great hope

My 1st was on approval
Then in a book I saw
The words that I had written
I could not ask for more

Caroline Halliday

My Knight

Once I was a princess
With a cardboard crown,
Once you were a knight
And before me bowed down.
Once we were wrapped in innocence,
And protected by purity.
Once we lived in a magical world,
Just you my knight, and me.

Gail Lawson

First Love

I remember you, as if it was yesterday
Nursemaids and children in the park
   On the first day of our holiday
   I saw you first under a palm tree

Sun-bleached hair blowing across your forehead
You watch me play hide and seek
I was five and you were seven
A cluster of dates hung above your head

   Please, would you climb the tree, for me.
   You said: Yes, dates, for a kiss!

You chased, but could not catch me, how we ran
Round, and round those palm trees,
But at sundown an air-raid hit our town
The first one

   And you were the first one to die
   Never to claim a first kiss.

   N Bowden

My First Love

I met her on June 24th 2000
At a party I arranged, she was the friend of a friend
Glancing across the room, a deep impact!
Instinct overcoming trepidation I asked;
'So, what's your name?'

Within moments, we lay in the open air,
Under the setting summer sun, emitting breaths of amour
Gazing into her dark gorgeously radiant eyes,
Indescribably feelings swept over,
As a tender love song soared like a flame within us
Was this my chance for an infinite relationship?
Hand in hand as one, we made our way inside.

Arms around her, swaying slowly to the music,
Head against my shoulder,
As I cupped her face in my hands,
Our lips met affectionately
Gradually nuzzling her divinely smooth splendant neck,
I became enamoured with passion
This new sensation sparked a flame inside
My first love; a special companion
All in that evening calm and holy hour.

Nearly a year has passed, and no longer lovers
I see my companion occasionally,
But the fire within still blazes fondly,
As she holds a special place in my heart.

Stuart Cook

The Letter

An old lady had a letter written by her son
Telling her his inner thoughts of his life she had begun
He wanted her to know how much he really loved and cared
And appreciated all she'd done and the precious times they'd shared
It meant so much for him to let his deep emotions show
How much he thought about her in a way that she would know.

When his mother saw the letter and read it the first time
It filled her heart with pleasure and made her feel sublime
But sadly, after a little while, her mind will soon forget
For it can't retain the memory and all is lost, but yet,
When she rediscovers her letter and reads it again sometime
It fills her heart with the pleasure as if it was for that first time

Pauline Cunningham

Pen To Paper

I put my pen to paper
It's really just to say
There's a jewel of an isle
In a silver sea the beautiful
'Isle of Tresco'.

As I sit by my window
What do I see
Chimneys smoking as black as can be
This rat race I'd quit and
I'd hop on a ship for the beautiful
'Isle of Tresco'.

I'd there spend my days
Just watching the waves
Lap the beautiful shores of Tresco
After all's said and done
There is only one beautiful
'Isle of Tresco'
With no cars, no comet, and no Tesco.

E M Brooks

This Girl Of Mine

I am not a poet or literary man
But I'll put in words the best I can
I have a good wife, who has always done her best
So it's about our love, as you might have guessed

We met when she was seventeen and I loved her so
I was a service man so to war I had to go
We got engaged a year later on
She said 'Yes' and again I was gone

Twelve months passed and we were married at last
Then back to the war and flew out East very fast
I in India, longing for her with every breath I drew
My wife in England was lonely but faithful and true

I wrote to her as often as I could
And told her I loved her and always would
She saved up her money and my pay to her I sent
For our plans of having a home, all our efforts were spent

We got that home, furniture, as in our plan
And loved each other as only young ones can
Five years after our marriage, with a wish to fulfil
That was to make our love and bond stronger still

A son was born and brought us much joy
Five years later, another, planned baby, another lovely boy
What thrilling times these children brought
Along with greater love and so much happiness caught

We are now old and the young flaming passion is no more
But the love and bond is much deeper than ever before
I owe my life's happiness to this girl of mine
And hope that it will continue for a very long time

John Nelson

Her First Job

Ann found a job.
After months without.
The money was too neat.
Her friend said,
How difficult it was
For her to make ends meet.
Ann said, it was harder for her than that,
She found it such a bother:
She would only be too pleased,
If her ends could wave to each other.

Marijke

That Exhibition

Following intense years, graduating with honours,
Father, never too keen on my choice,
Certainly managed a warm handshake and smile;
Those days, art in his eyes seemed besmirched
Such intense male observing of nude female bodies!

At the presentation day, introduced to notable personages
Family reserve switched to public warmth of approval,
Of course, they'd nurtured me during the anxious years;
A name in a paper, otherwise, life just normal,
We, a quiet family, wholly united, father sat for a chalk portrait!

Now, no time to lose, I professionally framed dad's face
Expressing all its full detail
Deeply impressing his Edwardian significance;
So, we family hung it in a morning - obvious position,
Then it gradually lost its significance.

Then, noting the local paper, announcement, art exhibition,
Some little distance away - Preston.
Sending in day, I teetered with excitement,
Cycling with the drawing, secure on the carrier,
Then, days of anticipating the postman.

Yes, a letter from Preston, it was accepted!
So, we hired a car, Mum, Dad and I, for 'varnishing day'
On entering the crowded art gallery,
Personally received by the Mayor;
'Gladys, Gladys' he yelled across the gallery, 'He's here: He's here!'

James Lucas

The First Space Shuttle

I remember well the first shuttle,
Being launched into space.
And the heroism of those first astronauts,
Who weren't sure of the dangers they faced.
They had to be faithful and have plenty of pluck,
As it so happened they were given plenty of luck.
It was to be a never to be forgotten trip,
No-one could afford to make a slip.
Luckily it all went very well.
So there is really very little to tell.

Betty Green

First Crush (Dreams)

In my dreams you stroke my hair,
Whisper words to show you care,
Hold me close and still my fears,
Touch my hopes and kiss my tears.

In my dreams we are as one,
No-one to stop what's now begun.
You tell me all the things, I die to hear,
All distances breached, you are here.

In my dreams there's no beginning, no end,
You're my lover, my protector, my friend,
You hold me close and we let this be,
In my dreams you are here with me.

Emmalene Maguire

The Inevitable

Thank you for showing me what love is,
  The laughter, the beauty and of course all the bliss,
Thank you for loving me; if only for a while
  For sharing with me your wonderful smile,
Thank you for the memories
  I know someday I will cherish,
For the courage to admit, that for you
  The love was beginning to perish,
What you knew would never last
  No matter how hard.

My first love you will always be,
But to face the truth - the inevitable
It's up to me.
Time heals; I hope so
But remember always
You once made someone happy,
Made them realise that life was worthwhile,
And when you think of me . . .
Do so please with your wonderful smile . . .

  Aisling McGann

First Love

He was my first love,
Tall, dark, handsome in my eyes.
So we married. One did.
Our honeymoon was - different.
My love had become a runner
(One of his sudden fancies)
So I stood, stopwatch in hand,
Waiting for him to thunder
Out of the mist,
For this was December, in Dovedale.
Slowly realisation dawned.
Marriage, a wife, children, running,
Were all short lived hobbies,
To be superseded by mistresses
And one night stands.

And so my love died.
Divorce withers even lingering regrets.
He wanted his freedom, his life.
I wanted the children,
So that suited us both.
And them.

My first love became a lost love,
Giving his love to others.
Until they, in turn, lost it.

Ann Harrison

My Children So Far Away

The first sight I would have might be
A baby in my arms.
In no time he would talk to me
And melt me with his charms.

Another pink, bouncy bundle
Might be a little girl,
Who'd maybe gift a precious cuddle
Or toss a golden curl.

Then how do I describe this one?
Fast and very true,
Not only in the way he'd run,
But in how beautiful he grew.

They seemed to many other folk
Such a great big brood to love,
But I can always bank
On them when push comes to shove.

Fae D Watson

Ben
(Dedicated to Ben Jones)

You simply walked into the room
   And the room became transcendent
Your impact left me breathless
   While your talent stole my voice

With esteem I viewed your art
   While you spoke of Eric's Tones
Those pictures punched my core
   You were oblivious to my awe

Each expression still lives in me
   Lucid visions of sight and sound
Your laughter's my private melody
   My heart pines with every thought

Every day your image greets me
   A thousand times I play the scene
A million wishes pollute my dreamscape
   An insistent longing thrives within

Amid this vortex I now reside
   Of your voice, laughter and eyes
All still burning in my mind
   A blazing train of gifted insight

Let the day be with me soon
   Where all these fantasies evolve
So in your presence once again
   I can tell you of this love

Samantha Rees

216

My First, My Last

My thoughts of you sweep back across the years
Layered cobwebs fall away
Your eyes, your smile . . . my excitement just being *near*
I return again to that same reality . . . unchanged, even now . . . today

I knew you first when just a girl
And, how I loved you . . . even then
Who'd have dreamed you'd walk back into my world?
Who'd have dreamed I'd love you . . . still? . . . Again!

Now, I think of only you thru every endless day
And thru every endless night
Hoping somehow to find the way
To be together . . . and make this right

I truly believe . . . that I belong with you
And, that you truly belong with me
The bonds between us linger intense and true
Revealing a truth that's plain to see

We've weathered our times of ups and downs
We've weathered anger and dismay
Still, our passion lives and stands its ground
We've tried to go . . . but, yet we stay

Unable to break the connection
Unable to break the tie
Wanting only to touch each other
And, if that's not true love . . . then . . . why?

My heart and soul belong to only you
You're my lover . . . you're my friend
How can I live without you, what can I do?
My love's still . . . yours . . . without an end.

Mary Beth Bott

217

Our First True Love

Mummy! Oh Mummy do look!
At the most beautiful rainbow!
Spanning the brook, to make it look
'Like a gateway to heaven'

Please, could I make a wish?
Not for myself, but for the others!
For all the children's mothers,
Who, when things go wrong,
Open their arms like a pair of soft wings.
To make our troubles, into tiny things.
A big hug, dear mums,
To thank you for opening your arms.

From all you big and small chums.

Erika Rollinson

First And Last Love Of All
(To Dave with all my heart,
and for you girls too)

At sixteen we met,
I knew it was then,
what love meant,
you took my heart,
held it tight,
for us never to part,
since that day we met,
you were tall and dark,
I was small and fair,
you showed me how,
much life had to share.

Yet years have passed,
highs and lows,
come and go,
still, together we go,
a marriage,
two daughters,
two dogs and horse called Bo.

We laugh,
we cry,
we look on at our girls,
full of love and pride,
forever together,
till the day,
we die,
for us was the first,
the last love of all.

T A Peachey

My First Love

My first love was kept quiet
It was the most special thing I had ever felt
But I had to keep it deep inside
No-one could know
Not even the person I felt so strongly about
Could know my deep feelings
Life is too risky to say just what you want
There's too many rules
Too many boundaries
Too many lines to stay inside
I had to keep it in my own mind
Crying myself to sleep
The tears of lonely love drowned me
I'd give everything just to say
I love you
But I knew it would upset a lot of people
I had to get to liberty
So staring at the midnight stars for many nights
Helped the forbidden love fly away.

Stephanie Haley (15)

Poet's Corner

I've struggled now for many months
to write with wit and style.
To capture what I'm looking for
has taken quite a while.
At last I feel I'm coming close,
some verse is almost good.
Send them to a publisher?
Kind critics say I should.
So plucking up my courage,
I posted them away,
and then sat back and waited
for a triumphant day.
But with no response forthcoming,
my hopes began to die.
They obviously weren't good enough
to warrant a reply.
But after weeks of waiting,
I feel I've made the trip.
At last I'm a real writer,
with my first rejection slip!

Bill Baker

Hello, My Baby

Hi, Mom, here I am - It's been a long nine months,
Sometimes you couldn't eat,
Then I kicked you with my feet,
Sometimes you couldn't sleep
Or I woke you up from slumber deep.

Hi, Mom, here I am - The waiting's finally over,
I know I'm welcome in our family,
I'm glad that you're my mother,
When you cuddle me in you arms
I wouldn't choose another.

Hi, Mom, here I am - I love the feel of your touch
When you count my tiny toes and fingers,
I know you'll teach me much
About life, and God, and such -
Good examples tend to linger.

Hi, Mom, here I am - I'm comforted by your singing
Sweet lullabies when I cry,
I hope we will always be
As close as I'm now clinging,
Though at times we'll disagree.

Hi, Mom, here I am - I'll be your constant companion,
We'll be friends when I grow up,
I know you'll never abandon me when I am needy
For I'm your firstborn baby.

Hello, my baby - I'm so glad that you are here,
Now I know how motherhood feels,
The keenest of all senses,
What millions of mothers before me felt
When they first held their child.
I will see, touch, feel, hold, love and keep you forever.

Floriana Hall

An Móinín Agus Sinéad

In the early hours of the morning
the gardí arrived to close the bar
and while doing so of course
ordered a jar each for themselves
as last-minute-refilled jugs passed
beneath the sign reading
No glasses in the ballroom please.

Suddenly she turned and asked me if I'd like to dance.
Slow dance - 16 verses 24 - me trembling unmanly - the first time
with a woman in my arms.
No seats left. I offered the only vacant one to her.
She smiled. 'I won't hog it for myself but - hey, sure let's not waste it.
You have the chair - and if you don't mind - might I sit
on your *lap* instead?'

It wasn't the beer or music - it was the comfortable
weight of her, the soft and slender arm around my neck
and the dizzy spell of her scent that took a short cut through
my senses. The affectionate eyes, the warm open smile; soft dark hair
brushing my face - the risen hem of her short peach dress
intoxicating my astonished, stunned, hardly-able-to-believe-it
adolescent head.

The next day hand in hand we walked the blackbird singing Moneen
away from the inquisitive eyes of a small conversational Kildare town.
Momentarily we lost ourselves in an *interminable* kiss - my
heart exploding,
the bits and pieces descending into the belly dancing fire like
wayward
sparks consumed by the sort of love so far only dreamt of.

A few moments of non-existence followed, nursed back by
contented caresses. Deliverance out of nowhere, like waking from
a dream.
Sunlight streamed through sentinel trees. A vista opened up in
which hope
sprang eternal, exhilarating and solar warm; me thinking: *life at last
has just begun!*
In the golden glow of new found treasure there was no hint of
the future -
no hint of anything but love. Certainly no clues about the years
of dark and tangled emotional webs waiting to be spun.

Pat McGrath

My First

Such happy thoughts filled my head
On the day when I first wed,
A cosy home with children there
A partner to love and share.
Within one year I became a mum
That was when my heartache began,
My partner left me for another,
She was the wife of his own brother.
I felt my world had fallen apart
And I would die of a broken heart,
But when I looked at my twin boys,
My heartache always turned to joy.
Life was hard but I got by,
No longer did I sit and cry,
Time slipped by - fate took a hand,
Now I wore a second gold band,
This time I was happy and content,
Fifteen years together we spent.
Then came a sudden end,
I lost my partner - my best friend,
Many years since then have flown,
But true happiness I had known.
Though my first time I'll never forget,
My second time holds no regrets.

Olive Godfrey